OXFORD STUDENT TEXTS
Series Editor: Victor Lee

✳

Six
Women Poets

✳

Edited by Judith Kinsman

Oxford University Press

for Celia

Oxford University Press, Great Clarendon Street, Oxford OX2 6DP

Oxford New York
Athens Auckland Bangkok Bogota Bombay
Buenos Aires Calcutta Cape Town Dar es Salaam
Delhi Florence Hong Kong Istanbul Karachi
Kuala Lumpur Madras Madrid Melbourne
Mexico City Nairobi Paris Singapore
Taipei Tokyo Toronto

and associated companies in
Berlin Ibadan

Oxford is a trade mark of Oxford University Press

© Selection and notes: Judith Kinsman 1992
First published by Oxford University Press 1992
Sixth impression 1997
ISBN 0 19 833181 9

Printed and bound by
Butler & Tanner Ltd, Frome and London

Other titles in the series

Blake: Songs of Innocence and of Experience	0 19 831952 5
Chaucer: General Prologue to the Canterbury Tales	0 19 831967 3
Chaucer: The Nun's Priest's Tale	0 19 831987 8
Chaucer: The Miller's Tale	0 19 831988 6
John Donne: Selected Poems	0 19 831950 9
Christopher Fry: The Lady's Not for Burning	0 19 831959 2
Gerard Manley Hopkins: Selected Poems	0 19 831961 4
D. H. Lawrence: Selected Poems	0 19 831962 2
Alexander Pope: The Rape of the Lock	0 19 831958 4
William Wordsworth: Selected Poems	0 19 831951 7
W. B. Yeats: Selected Poems	0 19 831966 5

Contents

Acknowledgements

Fleur Adcock: 'Earlswood', 'Loving Hitler', 'Outwood', 'Tadpoles', 'For Heidi with Blue Hair', 'The Telephone Call', 'The Chiffonier', 'The Keepsake', 'Witnesses', and 'Last Song' from *The Incident Book* (1986); 'Nature Table', 'The Prize-winning Poem', and 'Street Song' from *Selected Poems* (1983). Reprinted by permission of Oxford University Press.

Gillian Clarke: 'Letter From A Far Country', 'Login', 'Scything', 'Siege', 'East Moors', and 'White Roses' from *Letter From A Far Country*; 'Miracle on St David's Day', 'The Sundial', 'Marged', 'Overheard in County Sligo', 'Last Rites', and 'Still Life' from *Selected Poems*. Reprinted by permission of Carcanet Press Limited.

Selima Hill: 'Chicken Feathers', 'The Ram', 'Dewpond and Black Drainpipes', 'The Flowers', 'Down by the Salley Gardens', 'Among the Thyme and Daisies', 'The Goose', 'The Bicycle Ride', 'Below Hekla', and extract from 'The Fowlers of the Marshes' all from *Saying Hello At The Station* (Chatto, 1984); 'Diving at Midnight' from *My Darling Camel* (Chatto). Reprinted by permission of Random Century Group.

Liz Lochhead: 'The Offering', 'The Teachers', 'The Prize', 'Revelation', 'Poppies', 'An Abortion', 'Laundrette', 'A Giveaway', 'The Other Woman', 'Spinster', 'Storyteller', 'The Father', 'The Mother', 'Everybody's Mother' all from *Dreaming Frankenstein* (1987); 'Fat Girl's Confession' from *True Confessions*. Reprinted by permission of Polygon.

Grace Nichols: from 'Caribbean Woman Prayer', © Grace Nichols 1988. Reprinted by permission of Curtis Brown on behalf of Grace Nichols; 'Waterpot', 'Sugar Cane', 'We the Women', 'I Coming Back', 'Ala', 'In My Name' and 'Like a Flame' from *I Is A Long Memoried Woman*. Reprinted by permission of Karnak House; 'Praise Song For My Mother', 'Be a Butterfly', 'Iguana Memory', and 'Waiting for Thelma's Laughter' from *Fat Black Woman's Poems*. Reprinted by permission of Virago Press; 'Those Women' first published AMBIT; 'Up my spine', 'Of course they ask for poems about the "Realities" of Black Women' from *A Dangerous Knowing* (Sheba Feminist Publishers, 1985), © Grace Nichols 1985.

Carol Rumens: all from *Selected Poems* (Chatto & Windus). Reprinted by permission of Random Century Group.

Every effort has been made to secure permissions prior to publication. If contacted the publisher will be pleased to rectify any errors or omissions at the earliest opportunity.

The cover illustration is by John Rushton. It was drawn from photographs originally supplied by: Susan Butler (top left, Gillian Clarke), Fanny Dubes (top middle, Grace Nichols), Caroline Forbes (top right, Fleur Adcock), Fay Goodwin/Network Photographers (bottom left, Carol Rumens), David West (bottom middle, Selima Hill), The Scotsman Publications Ltd (bottom right, Liz Lochhead).

Editors

Dr Victor Lee

Dr Victor Lee, the Series Editor, read English at University College, Cardiff. He was awarded a doctorate at Oxford University. He has experience of teaching at Secondary and Tertiary level, and is currently working at the Open University. Victor Lee has been Chief Examiner in English for three examination boards over a period of twenty years.

Judith Kinsman

Judith Kinsman read English and American Literature at the University of East Anglia and has taught English in Avon and Somerset schools for the last seventeen years. In that time, she has set up writers' residencies in schools and in the community and organized writing courses for students. These have involved her working closely with many contemporary writers. She is currently Head of English at Cotham Grammar School in Bristol and has recently become an A level examiner.

Foreword

Oxford Student Texts are specifically aimed at presenting poetry and drama to an audience which is studying English Literature at an advanced level. *Six Women Poets* is something of a departure, being the first anthology to be included in the series, and an anthology which draws together some of the best contemporary women's poetry. As usual, the poetry is placed first to encourage students to develop their own response to it and to enjoy it without secondary critical material of any kind. An interesting addition has been made in that the selections from all six poets are prefaced by an introduction written in each case by the poet herself, and providing an accessible way in to the poems.

The second and third parts of *Six Women Poets* offer support, where this is necessary, through critical readings of the poems. The Notes section performs the function of giving explanations for specific lines and allusions. The Reviews section, raises themes for consideration and issues for response. One of the major aims of this part of the text is to emphasize that there is no one right answer to interpretation, but rather a series of approaches. Readers are provided with critical material, but left to make up their own minds as to which are the most suitable interpretations or to hold their own.

A list of Further Reading for all six poets is given at the end of the text, together with Tasks intended to help in the exploration of ideas after the poems have been read and the Notes and Reviews studied. These Tasks should prove helpful for coursework projects or in preparing for an examination.

Victor Lee *Series Editor*

The Poems

Gillian Clarke
The Poet's Introduction

Letter from a Far Country is a letter from a fictitious woman to all men. The 'far country' is childhood, womanhood, Wales, the beautiful country where the warriors, kings and presidents don't live, the private place where we all grow up.

Most women on earth are powerless to decide, to choose or to change society, yet the creative contribution of anonymous women to the history of the world is immeasurably vast. As I write, low-flying military jets shatter the country morning silence, the milk tanker man has driven past, the postman has been and on the radio a man is reading the news. Where are the women? The wife. Mrs Somebody. Miss Anonymous. Where have they been and what have they been doing since the evolution of humankind? 'Where,' as the foolish man quoted in *Letter* asked me, 'are their great works?' It is as if the earth – birth, death, caring, nurturing, teaching, nursing, home-making, were in women's hands, while the world – public life, money, government, organization, judgement, war, were in the hands of men. This would, perhaps, suit us well enough, if only both kinds of work were equally valued, but we all know they are not. It's Hercules, Hitler and Napoleon we've heard of, not the embroiderers, cheesemakers, story-tellers and singers of nursery rhymes.

In a way *Letter* is my small contribution towards feminist protest, a meditation on traditional woman's work written in the form of an imaginary letter, the sort of letter you write in your mind and never post. At the same time it is a celebration of life's good things – clean sheets, the smell of baking, orderliness – with which my mother and grandmother surrounded me. It draws on history, parish registers, census lists, nursery rhymes and the compost-heap of the mind for its imagery, and the place is a real Welsh parish. It was commissioned by the BBC as a half-hour radio poem, and I wrote it easily in

1

between 10 and 15 hours spread over five late-night sessions when my sons' drums and guitars had fallen silent for the night.

The Sundial, written twenty-two years ago, when my son Owain was six, was the first poem I had written since being a student, and my first published poem. Owain had a feverish nightmare. Next day I anxiously watched him make his sundial, mother and child caged in a suburban garden, with the lion-sun-clock pointing its menacing stick-shadow at us. It marked time passing and a boy growing up all too quickly into a threatening world.

Several of the poems in this selection are elegies, poems about death, ending or loss: the willow warbler's eggs in *Scything*; Marged's suicide over 60 years ago in my cottage; the closing of East Moors steelworks; the twenty-year-old motor cyclist in *Last Rites*; the 11-year-old son of a friend in *White Roses*. Dylan, who shared the sorrow in *Scything*, is my younger son. Marged is the woman who, in *Letter*, lived in poverty in the 'innocent smallholding' in which I now live in modernized comfort.

All my poems are true stories. *Siege* was the Iranian embassy siege of the early 1980s, which came to a violent end witnessed live on radio and television. In the poem I try to blend three elements: the distant violence, the beauty of my garden, and memories stirred by a box of old photographs. At the time, I lived in the house I was born in. In such moments of extreme feeling, past and present, faraway and close things, seem to fuse into a single fierce experience.

They fuse, I hope, the daffodils' silence, the thrush's song, and the voice of the dumb man speaking a poem in *Miracle on St David's Day*; the present, past and future in *Login*, (the name of the village where my grandmother's farm was, and where my father and the woman in the poem had been young and, my son and I suddenly realized, had loved each other); the beauty of summer and the horror of a fatal road accident in *Last Rites*.

Writing is work, and a writer should be able to tackle any word-task. I write articles, book reviews, editorials, even, once, a Valentine for someone to send her boss as a joke. Once in a while, however, I'm a poet. I might be driving, falling asleep, digging the garden, walking my spaniel, reading, listening to music, and a poem will nudge me. I feel alert, my heart beats a little faster, and I must take up my pen. This mood may last an hour, or many weeks, and in its grip I write obsessively, at the expense of other duties. Often I seek this mood deliberately, fill pages with words like drawing, seeing where words will lead. If all goes well the page fills quickly, and after one draft or twenty, there it is, brand-new and as good as I can make it.

The poet is the voice of the tribe, with responsibilities to language and to people, and poetry's purpose is to give words to all human experience, and thus to share it.

Letter from a Far Country

They have gone. The silence resettles
slowly as dust on the sunlit
surfaces of the furniture.
At first the skull itself makes
sounds in any fresh silence,
a big sea running in a shell.
I can hear my blood rise and fall.

Dear husbands, fathers, forefathers,
this is my apologia, my
10   letter home from the future,
my bottle in the sea which might
take a generation to arrive.

The morning's all activity.
I draw the detritus of a family's
loud life before me, a snow plough,
a road-sweeper with my cart of leaves.
The washing-machine drones
in the distance. Frome time to time
as it falls silent I fill baskets
20   with damp clothes and carry them
into the garden, hang them out,
stand back, take pleasure counting
and listing what I have done.
The furniture is brisk with polish.
On the shelves in all of the rooms
I arrange the books
in alphabetical order
according to subject: Mozart,
Advanced Calculus, William,
30   and Paddington Bear.

Into the drawers I place your clean
clothes, pyjamas with buttons
sewn back on, shirts stacked neatly
under their labels on the shelves.

The chests and cupboards are full,
the house sweet as a honeycomb.
I move in and out of the hive
all day, harvesting, ordering.
You will find all in its proper place,
40   when I have gone.

As I write I am far away.
First see a landscape. Hill country,
essentially feminine,
the sea not far off. Bryn Isaf
down there in the crook of the hill
under Calfaria's single eye.
My grandmother might have lived there.
Any farm. Any chapel.
Father and minister, on guard,
50   close the white gates to hold her.

A stony track turns between
ancient hedges, narrowing,
like a lane in a child's book.
Its perspective makes the heart restless
like the boy in the rhyme, his stick
and cotton bundle on his shoulder.

The minstrel boy to the war has gone.
But the girl stays. To mind things.
She must keep. And wait. And pass time.

60 There's always been time on our hands.
    We read this perfectly white page
    for the black head of the seal,
    for the cormorant, as suddenly gone
    as a question from the mind,
    snaking underneath the surfaces.
    A cross of gull shadow on the sea
    as if someone stepped on its grave.
    After an immeasurable space
    the cormorant breaks the surface
70 as a small, black, returning doubt.

    From here the valley is narrow,
    the lane lodged like a halfway ledge.
    From the opposite wood the birds
    ring like a tambourine. It's not
    the birdsong of a garden, thrush
    and blackbird, robin and finch,
    distinguishable, taking turn.
    The song's lost in saps and seepings,
    amplified by hollow trees,
80 cupped leaves and wind in the branches.
    All their old conversations
    collected carefully, faded
    and difficult to read, yet held
    forever as voices in a well.

    Reflections and fallen stones; shouts
    into the scared dark of lead-mines;
    the ruined warehouse where the owls stare;
    sea-caves; cellars; the back stairs
    behind the chenille curtain;
90 the landing when the lights are out;
    nightmares in hot feather beds;
    the barn where I'm sent to fetch Taid;

that place where the Mellte flows
boldly into limestone caves
and leaps from its hole a mile on,
the nightmare still wild in its voice.

When I was a child a young boy
was drawn into a pipe and drowned
at the swimming pool. I never
100   forgot him, and pity rivers
inside mountains, and the children
of Hamelin sucked in by music.
You can hear children crying
from the empty woods.
It's all given back in concert
with the birds and leaves and water
and the song and dance of the Piper.

Listen! to the starlings glistening
on a March morning! Just one day
110   after snow, an hour after frost,
the thickening grass begins to shine
already in the opening light.
There's wind to rustle the blood,
the sudden flame of crocus.

My grandmother might be standing
in the great silence before the Wars,
hanging the washing between trees
over the white and the red hens.
Sheets, threadworked pillowcases.
120   Mamgu's best pais, her Sunday frock.

The sea stirs restlessly between
the sweetness of clean sheets,
the lifted arms,
the rustling petticoats.

My mother's laundry list, ready
on Mondays when the van called.
The rest soaked in glutinous starch
and whitened with a bluebag
kept in a broken cup.

130 (In the airing cupboard you'll see
a map, numbering and placing
every towel, every sheet.
I have charted all your needs.)

It has always been a matter
of lists. We have been counting,
folding, measuring, making,
tenderly laundering cloth
ever since we have been women.

The waves are folded meticulously,
140 perfectly white. Then they are tumbled
and must come to be folded again.

Four herring gulls and their shadows
are shouting at the clear glass
of a shaken wave. The sea's a sheet
bellying in the wind, snapping.
Air and white linen. Our airing cupboards
are full of our satisfactions.

The gulls grieve at our contentment.
It is a masculine question.
150 'Where' they call 'are your great works?'
They slip their fetters and fly up
to laugh at land-locked women.
Their cries are cruel as greedy babies.

Our milky tendernesses dry
to crisp lists; immaculate
linen; jars labelled and glossy
with our perfect preserves.
Spiced oranges; green tomato
chutney; Seville orange marmalade
160 annually staining gold
the snows of January.

(The saucers of marmalade
are set when the amber wrinkles
like the sea if you blow it.)

Jams and jellies of blackberry,
crabapple, strawberry, plum,
greengage and loganberry.
You can see the fruit pressing
their little faces against the glass;
170 tiny onions imprisoned
in their preservative juices.

Familiar days are stored whole
in bottles. There's a wet morning
orchard in the dandelion wine;
a white spring distilled
in elderflower's clarity;
and a loving, late, sunburning
day of October in syrups
of rose hip and the beautiful
180 black sloes that stained the gin to rose.

It is easy to make of love
these ceremonials. As priests
we fold cloth, break bread, share wine,
hope there's enough to go round.

(You'll find my inventories pinned
inside all of the cupboard doors.)

Soon they'll be planting the barley.
I imagine I see it, stirring
like blown sand, feel the stubble
190   cutting my legs above blancoed
daps in a summer too hot
for Wellingtons. The cans of tea
swing squeakily on wire loops,
outheld, not to scald myself,
over the ten slow leagues
of the field of golden knives.
To be out with the men, at work,
I had longed to carry their tea,
for the feminine privilege,
200   for the male right to the field.
Even that small task made me bleed.
Halfway between the flowered lap
of my grandmother and the black
heraldic silhouette of men
and machines on the golden field.
I stood crying, my ankle bones
raw and bleeding like the poppies
trussed in the corn stooks in their torn
red silks and soft mascara blacks.

210   (The recipe for my best bread,
half granary meal, half strong brown flour,
water, sugar, yeast and salt,
is copied out in the small black book.)

In the black book of this parish
a hundred years ago

you will find the unsupported
woman had 'pauper' against her name.
She shared it with old men.

The parish was rich with movement.
220   The woollen mills were spinning.
Water-wheels milled the sunlight
and the loom's knock was a heart
behind all activity.
The shuttles were quick as birds
in the warp of the oakwoods.
In the fields the knives were out
in a glint of husbandry.
In back bedrooms, barns and hedges,
in hollows of the hills,
230   the numerous young were born.

The people were at work:
dressmaker; wool carder; quilter;
midwife; farmer; apprentice;
house servant; scholar; labourer;
shepherd; stocking knitter; tailor;
carpenter; mariner; ploughman;
wool spinner; cobbler; cottager;
Independent Minister.

And the paupers: Enoch Elias
240   and Ann, his wife; David Jones,
Sarah and Esther their daughter;
Mary Evans and Ann Tanrallt;
Annie Cwm March and child;
Eleanor Thomas, widow, Cryg Glas;
Sara Jones, 84, and daughter;
Nicholas Rees, aged 80, and his wife;

Mariah Evans the Cwm, widow;
on the parish for want of work.
Housebound by infirmity, age,
250 widowhood, or motherhood.
Before the Welfare State who cared
for sparrows in a hard spring?

The stream's cleaner now; it idles
past derelict mill-wheels; the drains
do its work. Since the tanker sank
the unfolding rose of the sea
blooms on the beaches, wave on wave
black, track-marked, each tide
a procession of the dead.
260 Slack water's treacherous; each veined
wave is a stain in seal-milk;
the sea gapes, hopelessly
licking itself.

(Examine your hands
scrupulously
for signs of dirt in your own blood.
And wash them before meals.)

In that innocent smallholding
where the swallows live and field mice
270 winter and the sheep barge in
under the browbone, the windows
are blind, are doors for owls,
bolt-holes for dreams. The thoughts have flown.
The last death was a suicide.
The lowing cows discovered her,
the passing-bell of their need
warned a winter morning that day
when no one came to milk them.

Later, they told me, a baby
280 was born in the room where she died,
as if by this means sanctified,
a death outcried by a birth.
Middle-aged, poor, isolated,
she could not recover
from mourning an old parent's death.
Influenza brought an hour
too black, too narrow to escape.

More mysterious to them
was the woman who had everything.
290 A village house with railings;
rooms of good furniture;
fine linen in the drawers;
a garden full of herbs and flowers;
a husband in work; grown sons.
She had a cloud on her mind,
they said, and her death shadowed them.
It couldn't be explained.
I watch for her face looking out,
small and white, from every window,
300 like a face in a jar. Gossip,
whispers, lowing sounds. Laughter.

The people have always talked.
The landscape collects conversations
as carefully as a bucket,
gives them back in concert
with a wood of birdsong.

(If you hear your name in that talk
don't listen. Eavesdroppers never
heard anything good of themselves.)

310   When least expected you catch
      the eye of the enemy
      looking coldly from the old world...
      Here's a woman who ought to be
      up to her wrists in marriage;
      not content with the second hand
      she is shaking the bracelets
      from her arms. The sea circles
      her ankles. Watch its knots loosen
      from the delicate bones
320   of her feet, from the rope of foam
      about a rock. The seal swims
      in a collar of water
      drawing the horizon in its wake.
      And doubt breaks the perfect
      white surface of the day.

      About the tree in the middle
      of the cornfield the loop of gold
      is loose as water; as the love
      we should bear one another.

330   When I rock the sea rocks. The moon
      doesn't seem to be listening
      invisible in a pale sky,
      keeping a light hand on the rein.
      Where is woman in this trinity?
      The mare who draws the load?
      The hand on the leather?
      The cargo of wheat?

      Watching sea-roads I feel
      the tightening white currents,
340   am waterlogged, my time set
      to the sea's town clock.
      My cramps and drownings, energies,

desires draw the loaded net
of the tide over the stones.

A lap full of pebbles and then
light as a Coca Cola can.
I am freight. I am ship.
I cast ballast overboard.
The moon decides my Equinox.
350 At high tide I am leaving.

The women are leaving.
They are paying their taxes
and dues. Filling in their passports.
They are paying to Caesar
what is Caesar's, to God what is God's,
To Woman what is Man's.

I hear the dead grandmothers,
Mamgu from Ceredigion,
Nain from the North, all calling
360 their daughters down from the fields,
calling me in from the road.
They haul at the taut silk cords;
set us fetching eggs, feeding hens,
mixing rage with the family bread,
lock us to the elbows in soap suds.
Their sculleries and kitchens fill
with steam, sweetnesses, goosefeathers.

On the graves of my grandfathers
the stones, in their lichens and mosses,
370 record each one's importance.
Diaconydd. Trysorydd.
Pillars of their society.
Three times at chapel on Sundays.
They are in league with the moon

but as silently stony
as the simple names of their women.

We are hawks trained to return
to the lure from the circle's
far circumference. Children sing
380   that note that only we can hear.
The baby breaks the waters,
disorders the blood's tune, sets
each filament of the senses
wild. Its cry tugs at flesh, floods
its mother's milky fields.
Nightly in white moonlight I wake
from sleep one whole slow minute
before the hungry child
wondering what woke me.

390   School's out. The clocks strike four.
Today this letter goes unsigned,
unfinished, unposted.
When it is finished
I will post it from a far country.

If we launch the boat and sail away
Who will rock the cradle? Who will stay?
If women wander over the sea
Who'll be home when you come in for tea?

If we go hunting along with the men
400   *Who will light the fires and bake bread then?*
Who'll catch the nightmares and ride them away
If we put to sea and we sail away?

Will the men grow tender and the children strong?
Who will teach the Mam iaith and sing them songs?
If we adventure more than a day
Who will do the loving while we're away?

Miracle on St David's Day

'They flash upon that inward eye
Which is the bliss of solitude'
'The Daffodils' by W. Wordsworth

An afternoon yellow and open-mouthed
with daffodils. The sun treads the path
among cedars and enormous oaks.
It might be a country house, guests strolling,
the rumps of gardeners between nursery shrubs.

I am reading poetry to the insane.
An old woman, interrupting, offers
as many buckets of coal as I need.
A beautiful chestnut-haired boy listens
10   entirely absorbed. A schizophrenic

on a good day, they tell me later.
In a cage of first March sun a woman
sits not listening, not seeing, not feeling.
In her neat clothes the woman is absent.
A big, mild man is tenderly led

to his chair. He has never spoken.
His labourer's hands on his knees, he rocks
gently to the rhythms of the poems.
I read to their presences, absences,
20   to the big, dumb labouring man as he rocks.

He is suddenly standing, silently,
huge and mild, but I feel afraid. Like slow
movement of spring water or the first bird
of the year in the breaking darkness,
the labourer's voice recites 'The Daffodils'.

The nurses are frozen, alert; the patients
seem to listen. He is hoarse but word-perfect.
Outside the daffodils are still as wax,
a thousand, ten thousand, their syllables
30   unspoken, their creams and yellows still.

Forty years ago, in a Valleys school,
the class recited poetry by rote.
Since the dumbness of misery fell
he has remembered there was a music
of speech and that once he had something to say.

When he's done, before the applause, we observe
the flowers' silence. A thrush sings
and the daffodils are flame.

Login

Chapel and bridge. A headlong fall
into woods. A river running fast
divides the wild cow parsley.
'My father lived here once,' I said,
'I think you knew him.'

The sun, hot at our backs, whitens
the lane. She, in shadow, allows
the sun to pass her into the passage.
I gain entry at his name, tea,
10 a lace cloth on the table.

When talking is done she ruffles
my son's brown hair with a hand
that is bruised with age. Veins stand,
fast water in her wrists. Handshakes,
glances converging could not span
such giddy water.

Out in the lane the thrush outsings
the river. The village is at lunch.
The bridge burns with cow parsley.
20 We stand in the brilliance without words,
watch him running into the light.

Should he turn now to wave and wait
for me, where sunlight concentrates
blindingly on the bridge, he'd see
all this in sepia, hear footsteps
not yet taken fade away.

The Sundial

Owain was ill today. In the night
He was delirious, shouting of lions
In the sleepless heat. Today, dry
And pale, he took a paper circle,
Laid it on the grass which held it
With curling fingers. In the still
Centre he pushed the broken bean
Stick, gathering twelve fragments
Of stone, placed them at measured
10   Distances. Then he crouched, slightly
Trembling with fever, calculating
The mathematics of sunshine.

He looked up, his eyes dark,
Intelligently adult as though
The wave of fever taught silence
And immobility for the first time.
Here, in his enforced rest, he found
Deliberation, and the slow finger
Of light, quieter than night lions,
20   More worthy of his concentration.
All day he told the time to me.
All day we felt and watched the sun
Caged in its white diurnal heat,
Pointing at us with its black stick.

Scything

It is blue May. There is work
to be done. The spring's eye blind
with algae, the stopped water
silent. The garden fills
with nettle and briar.
Dylan drags branches away.
I wade forward with my scythe.

There is stickiness on the blade.
Yolk on my hands. Albumen and blood.
10 Fragments of shell are baby-bones,
the scythe a scalpel, bloodied and guilty
with crushed feathers, mosses, the cut cords
of the grass. We shout at each other
each hurting with a separate pain.

From the crown of the hawthorn tree
to the ground the willow warbler
drops. All day in silence she repeats
her question. I too return
to the place holding the pieces,
20 at first still hot from the knife,
recall how warm birth fluids are.

Marged

I think of her sometimes when I lie in bed,
falling asleep in the room I have made in the roof-space
over the old dark parlŵr where she died
alone in winter, ill and penniless.
Lighting the lamps, November afternoons,
a reading book, whisky gold in my glass.
At my type-writer tapping under stars
at my new roof-window, radio tunes
and dog for company. Or parking the car
10   where through the mud she called her single cow
up from the field, under the sycamore.
Or looking at the hills she looked at too.
I find her broken crocks, digging her garden.
What else do we share, but being women?

Siege

I waste the sun's last hour, sitting here
at the kitchen window. Tea and a pile
of photographs to sort. Radio news
like smoke of conflagrations far away.
There isn't room for another petal
or leaf out there, this year of blossom.
Light dazzles the hedge roots underneath
the heavy shadows, burns the long grass.

10   *I, in my father's arms in this garden*
    with dandelion hair. He, near forty,
    unaccustomed to the restlessness
    of a baby's energy. Small hands
    tear apart the photograph's composure.
    She pushes his chest to be let down
    where daisies embroider his new shoes.

Perfumes and thorns are tearing
from the red may tree. Wild white Morello
and a weeping cherry heavy in flower.
The lilac slowly shows. Small oaks spread
20 their gestures. Poplars glisten. Pleated green
splits black husks of ash. Magnolia
drops its wax. Forsythia
fallen like a yellow dress.
Underfoot daisies from a deep
original root burst the darkness.

  My mother, posing in a summer dress
    in the corn at harvest time. Her brothers,
    shadowy middle distance figures,
    stoop with pitchforks to lift the sheaves.

30   *Out of sight Captain, or Belle, head fallen*
     to rest in the lee of the load, patient
     for the signal. Out of heart too the scare
     of the field far down from the sunstruck top
     of the load, and the lurch at the gate
     as we ditch and sway left down the lane.

The fallen sun lies low in the bluebells.
It is nearly summer. Midges hang
in the air. A wren is singing, sweet
in a lilac tree. Thrushes hunt the lawn,
40   eavesdrop for stirrings in the daisy roots.
The wren repeats her message distantly.
In a race of speedwell over grass
the thrushes are silently listening.
A yellow butterfly begins
its unsteady journey over the lawn.

The radio voices break and suddenly
the garden burns, is full of barking dogs.
A woman screams and gunsmoke blossoms
in the apple trees. Sheaves of fire
50   are scorching the grass and in my kitchen
is a roar of floors falling, machine guns.

The wren moves closer and repeats that song
of lust and burgeoning. Never clearer
the figures standing on the lawn, sharpnesses
of a yellow butterfly, almost there.

Overheard in County Sligo

I married a man from County Roscommon
and I live at the back of beyond
with a field of cows and a yard of hens
and six white geese on the pond.

At my door's a square of yellow corn
caught up by its corners and shaken,
and the road runs down through the open gate
and freedom's there for the taking.

I had thought to work on the Abbey stage
10 or have my name in a book,
to see my thought on the printed page,
or still the crowd with a look.

But I turn to fold the breakfast cloth
and to polish the lustre and brass,
to order and dust the tumbled rooms
and find my face in the glass.

I ought to feel I'm a happy woman
for I lie in the lap of the land,
and I married a man from County Roscommon
20 and I live in the back of beyond.

East Moors

At the end of a bitter April
the cherries flower at last in Penylan.
We notice the white trees and the flash
of sea with two blue islands beyond
the city, where the steelworks used to smoke.

I live in the house I was born in,
am accustomed to the sudden glow
of flame in the night sky, the dark sound
of something heavy dropped, miles off,
10   the smell of sulphur almost natural.

In Roath and Rumney now, washing strung
down the narrow gardens will stay clean.
Lethargy settles in front rooms and wives
have lined up little jobs for men to do.
At East Moors they closed the steelworks down.

A few men stay to see it through. Theirs
the bitterest time as rolling mills
make rubble. Demolition gangs
erase skylines whose hieroglyphs
20   recorded all our stories.

I am reminded of that Sunday
years ago when we brought the children
to watch two water cooling towers
blown up, recall the appalling void
in the sunlight, like a death.

On this first day of May an icy
rain is blowing through this town,
quieter, cleaner, poorer from today.
The cherries are in flower in Penylan.
30   Already over East Moors the sky whitens, blind.

Last Rites

During this summer of the long drought
The road to Synod Inn has kept
Its stigmata of dust and barley seed;

At the inquest they tell it again:
How the lorry tents us from the sun,
His pulse dangerous in my hands,
A mains hum only, no message
Coming through. His face warm, profiled
Against tarmac, the two-stroke Yamaha
10 Dead as a black horse in a war.
Only his hair moves and the sound
Of the parched grass and harebells a handspan
Away, his fear still with me like the scream
Of a jet in an empty sky.
I cover him with the grey blanket
From my bed, touch his face as a child
Who makes her favourites cosy.
His blood on my hands, his cariad in my arms.

Driving her home we share that vision
20 Over August fields dying of drought
Of the summer seas shattering
At every turn of Cardigan Bay
Under the cruel stones of the sun.

Still Life

It was good tonight
To polish brass with you,
Our hands slightly gritty
With Brasso, as they would feel
If we'd been in the sea, salty.
It was as if we burnished
Our friendship, polished it
Until all the light-drowning
Tarnish of deceit
10 Were stroked away. Patterns
Of incredible honesty
Delicately grew, revealed
Quite openly to the pressure
Of the soft, torn rag.
We made a yellow-gold
Still-life out of clocks,
Candlesticks and kettles.
My sadness puzzled you.
I rubbed the full curve
20 Of an Indian goblet,
Feeling its illusory
Heat. It cooled beneath
My fingers and I read
In the braille formality
Of pattern, in the leaf
And tendril and stylised tree,
That essentially each
Object remains cold,
Separate, only reflecting
30 The other's warmth.

White Roses

Outside the green velvet sitting room
white roses bloom after rain.
They hold water and sunlight
like cups of fine white china.

Within the boy who sleeps in my care
in the big chair the cold bloom
opens at terrible speed
and the splinter of ice moves

in his blood as he stirs in the chair.
10 Remembering me he smiles
politely, gritting his teeth
in silence on pain's red blaze.

A stick man in the ashes, his fires
die back. He is spars and springs.
He can talk again, gather
his cat to his bones. She springs

with a small cry in her throat, kneading
with diamond paws his dry
as tinder flesh. The least spark
20 of pain will burn him like straw.

The sun carelessly shines after rain.
The cat tracks thrushes in sweet
dark soil. And without concern
the rose outlives the child.

Grace Nichols

The Poet's Introduction

As a writer and poet I'm excited by language of course. I care about language, and maybe that is another reason why I write. It's the battle with language that I love, that striving to be true to the inner language of my voice, the challenge of trying to create something new. I like working in both Standard English and Creole. I tend to want to fuse the two tongues because I come from a background where the two worlds were constantly interacting, though Creole was regarded, obviously, as the inferior by the colonial powers when I was growing up.

I think this is one of the main reasons why many Caribbean poets, including myself, have reclaimed our language heritage and are now exploring it. It's a language our foremothers and forefathers struggled to create after losing their own languages on the plantations and we are saying it's a valid, vibrant language. We're no longer going to treat it with contempt or allow it to be misplaced. We just don't see Creole as a dialect of English even though the words themselves are English-based, because the structure, rhythm, and intonation are an influence of West African speech.

I don't think the only reason I use Creole in my poetry is to preserve it, however. I find it genuinely exciting. Some Creole expressions are very vivid and concise and have no equivalent in English. Poems like *Sugar Cane*, *Like a Flame*, *We the Women*, *I Coming Back*, *Up my Spine*, all make use of Creole. These poems, along with *Ala* and *In My Name*, are from my first cycle of poems, *I is a long-memoried Woman*, which owes its inspiration to a dream I had one night of a young African girl swimming from Africa to the Caribbean with a garland of flowers around her. When I woke up I interpreted the dream to mean that she was trying to cleanse the ocean of the pain and suffering that her ancestors had gone through in that crossing from Africa to the New World, in slavery.

One familiar visual image of Africa is that of women bearing waterpots on their heads, which requires a great sense of balance and poise. In the poem, *Waterpot*, this suggestion is carried forward so that even in slavery the woman carries herself with human dignity, as if she were bearing a waterpot on her head.

It's not surprising that I wrote the poem *Sugar Cane* in this cycle, since this was the crop behind the history of slavery in the Caribbean. Described as a 'sweet' crop with a 'bitter' history, sugarcane required cheap labour, and the profit-making plantation owners were prepared to exploit a system of slavery, even though countless lives were lost and brutalized. The long-memoried woman empathizes with *Sugar Cane* because it is the sugarcane's juice and the slave's blood that were exploited in the making of sugar.

In *I Coming Back* and *Up my Spine* there's a suggestion of supernatural power at work. The slave-woman is warning 'Massa' (slavemaster) that she will return even after death to haunt him. She's virtually casting a spell upon him, and with incantatory vengefulness she identifies with the 'skinless higue', a vampire-like figure in Caribbean folklore. In *Up my Spine* even the decrepit old woman, worn out by slavery, seems to have some supernatural trick up her sleeve. In order to survive the slaves had to resort to hidden resources of strength and defiance. It is said that some slave women even killed their newborn babies so as to spare them a destiny of slavery. In any case there was the belief that the souls would fly back to Africa free and perhaps even rejoin with Ala, the goddess who receives the dead back into the 'pocket' of her womb. However, the woman from the poem, *In My Name*, decides to keep her child ('her little bloodling').

Praise Song for My Mother, *Be a Butterfly*, *Iguana Memory*, and *Waiting for Thelma's Laughter* are all based on personal recollections. My mother liked laughing and I have this memory of her trying to restrain her laughter one day in church as the preacher was sweating it out and hysterically urging the congregation to be butterflies and not, as he put it, 'kyatta-pillas'.

Caribbean Woman Prayer was written shortly after a trip to the Caribbean during which I was struck by the grim economic deprivations underneath the colour and physical beauty of the landscape. I was also struck by the fact that many people seemed to have developed an almost fatalistic resignation and had turned to religion for solace. Watching the faces of her hungry children ('pickney') the woman is moved to seek divine help since political remedies have proved hopeless.

As someone from the Caribbean, I feel very multi-cultural and have been affected by all the different strands in that culture – African, Amerindian, Asian, European. I have a natural fear of anything that tries to close in on me, whether it is an ideology or a group of people who feel that we should all think alike because we're all women or because we're all black, and there is no room to accommodate anyone with a different view. In the early days when I first started reading my poems, mostly from *Long-memoried Woman*, a few women wanted to know why I wasn't focusing on the 'realities' of black women in this country – racial discrimination, bad housing etc. There is a great danger of stereotyping and limiting the lives of black people if we only see them as 'sufferers'. The poem, *Of course when they ask for poems about the Realities of black women*, affirms their complexity.

Waterpot

The daily going out
and coming in
always being hurried
along
like like… cattle

In the evenings
returning from the fields
she tried hard to walk
like a woman

10   she tried very hard
pulling herself erect
with every three or four
steps
pulling herself together
holding herself like
royal cane

And the overseer
hurrying them along
in the quickening darkness

20   And the overseer sneering
them along in the quickening
darkness
sneered at the pathetic
the pathetic display
of dignity

O but look
there's a waterpot growing
from her head

Sugar Cane

1
There is something
about sugar cane

he isn't what
he seem –

indifferent hard
and sheathed in blades

his waving arms
is a sign for help

his skin thick
10 only to protect
the juice inside
himself

2
His colour
is the aura
of jaundice
when he ripe

he shiver
like ague
when it rain

20 he suffer
from bellywork
burning fever
and delirium

just before
the hurricane
strike
smashing him to pieces

3
Growing up
is an art

he don't have   30
any control of

it is us
who groom and
weed him

who stick him
in the earth
in the first place

and when he
growing tall

with the help   40
of the sun
and rain

we feel the
need to strangle
the life

out of him

But either way he
    can't survive

4

Slowly
pain –
50   fully
sugar
cane
pushes
his
knotted
joints
upwards
from
the
60   earth
slowly
pain-
fully
he
comes
to learn
the
truth
about
70   himself
the
crimes
committed
in
his
name

5

He cast his shadow
to the earth

the wind is
his only mistress   80

I hear them
moving
in rustling tones

she shakes
his hard reserve

smoothing
stroking
caressing
all his length
shamelessly   90

I crouch
below them
quietly

Like a Flame

Raising up
from my weeding
of ripening cane

my eyes
make four
with this man

there ain't
no reason
to laugh

10   but
I laughing
in confusion

his hands
soft his words
quick his lips
curling as in
prayer

I nod

I like this man

20   Tonight
I go to meet him
like a flame

We the Women

We the women who toil
unadorn
heads tie with cheap
cotton

We the women who cut
clear fetch dig sing

We the women making
something from this
ache-and-pain-a-me
10   back-o-hardness

Yet we the women
who praises go unsung
who voices go unheard
who deaths they sweep
aside
as easy as dead leaves

I Coming Back

I coming back Massa
I coming back

mistress of the underworld
I coming back

colour and shape
of all that is evil
I coming back

dog howling outside
yuh window
10   I coming back

ball-a-fire
and skinless higue
I coming back

hiss in yuh ear
and prick in yuh skin
I coming back

bone in yuh throat
and laugh in yuh skull
I coming back

20   I coming back Massa
I coming back

Up my Spine

I see the old dry-head woman
leaning on her hoe
twist-up and shaky like a cripple insect

I see her ravaged skin
the stripes of mold
where the whip fall hard

I see her missing toe
her jut-out hipbone
from way back time when she had a fall

10   I see the old dry-head woman
leaning on her hoe
twist-up and shaky like a cripple insect

I see the pit of her eye

I hear her rattle bone laugh
putting a chill up my spine

Of course when they ask for poems about the 'Realities' of black women

what they really want
at times
is a specimen
whose heart is in the dust

a mother-of-sufferer
trampled/oppressed
they want a little black blood
undressed
and validation
10   for the abused stereotype
already in their heads

              or else they want
              a perfect song

I say I can write
no poem big enough
to hold the essence

              of a black woman
              or a white woman
              or a green woman

20   and there are black women
and black women
              like a contrasting sky
of rainbow spectrum

touch a black woman
you mistake for a rock
and feel her melting
down to fudge

cradle a soft black woman
and burn fingers as you trace
30 revolution
beneath her woolly hair

and yes we cut bush
to clear paths
for our children
and yes we throw sprat
to catch whale
and yes
if need be we'll trade
a piece-a-pussy
40 that see the pickney dem
in the grip-a-hungry-belly

still there ain't no
easy belly category

        for a black woman
        or a white woman
        or a green woman

and there are black women
strong and eloquent
and focused

50 and there are black women
who somehow always manage to end up
frail victim

and there are black women
considered so dangerous
in South Africa
they prison them away

        maybe this poem is to say

that I like to see
we black women
60 full-of-we-selves walking

        crushing out
        with each dancing step
the twisted self-negating
history
we've inherited

        crushing out
        with each dancing step

In My Name

Heavy with child

belly
an arc
of black moon

I squat over
dry plantain leaves

and command the earth
to receive you

in my name
10 in my blood

to receive you
my curled bean

my tainted

perfect child

my bastard fruit
my seedling
my sea grape
my strange mulatto
my little bloodling

20 Let the snake slipping in deep grass
be dumb before you

Let the centipede writhe and shrivel
in its tracks

Let the evil one strangle on his own tongue
even as he sets his eyes upon you

For with my blood
I've cleansed you
and with my tears
I've pooled the river Niger

30 now my sweet one it is for you to swim

Ala

Face up
they hold her naked body
to the ground
arms and legs spread-eagle
each tie with rope to stake

then they coat her in sweet
molasses and call us out
to see… the rebel woman

who with a pin
10   stick the soft mould
of her own child's head

sending the little new-born
soul winging its way back
to Africa – free

they call us out to see
the fate for all us rebel
women

the slow and painful
picking away of the flesh
20   by red and pitiless ants

but while the ants feed
and the sun blind her with
his fury
we the women sing and weep
as we work

O Ala
Uzo is due to join you
to return to the pocket
of your womb

30   Permit her remains to be
laid to rest – for she has
died a painful death

O Ala
Mother who gives and receives
again in death
Gracious one
have sympathy
let her enter
let her rest

Caribbean Woman Prayer

Wake up Lord
brush de sunflakes from yuh eye
back de sky a while Lord
an hear dis Mother-woman
on behalf of her pressure-down people

God de Mudder
God de Fadder
God de Sister
God de Brudder
10   God de Holy Fire

Ah don't need to tell yuh
how tings stan
cause right now you know
dat old lizard ah walk
lick land
an you know how de pickney belly laang
an you know how de fork ah hit stone
an tho it rain you know it really drought
an even now de man have start fuh count

20   de wata he make

God de Fadder
God de Mudder
God de Sister
God de Brudder
God de Holy Fire

Give me faith

O Lord
you know we is ah people
of a proud an generous heart
30   an how it shame us bad
dat we kyant welcome friend or stranger
when eat time come around

You know is not we nature
to behave like yard fowl

You know dat is de politics
an de times
an de tricks
dat has reduced we to dis

An talking bout politics Lord
40   I hope you give de politicians dem
de courage to do what they have to do
an to mek dem see dat tings must grow
from within
an not from without
even as you suffer us not
to walk in de rags of doubt

Mek dem see dat de people
must be at de root of de heart
dat dis place ain't Uncle Sam backyard
50   Lord, look how Rodney and Bishop get blast

God de Mudder
God de Fadder
God de Sister
God de Brudder
God de Holy Fire

To cut a laang story short
I want to see de children
wake up happy to de sunrise
an food in de pot

60   I want to see dem stretch limb
an watch dem sleep pon good stomach

I want to see de loss of hope
everywhere replace
wid de win of living

I want to see de man an woman
being in they being

Yes Lord
Halleliuh Lord!

All green tings an hibiscus praises Lord

Be a Butterfly

Don't be a kyatta-pilla
Be a butterfly
old preacher screamed
to illustrate his sermon
of Jesus and the higher life

rivulets of well-earned
sweat sliding down
his muscly mahogany face
in the half-empty school church
10 we sat shaking with muffling
laughter
watching our mother trying to save
herself from joining the wave

only our father remaining poker face
and afterwards we always went home to
split peas Sunday soup
with dumplings, fufu and pigtail

Don't be a kyatta-pilla
Be a butterfly
20 Be a butterfly

That was de life preacher
and you was right.

Those Women

Cut and contriving women
hauling fresh shrimps
up in their seines

standing waist deep
in the brown voluptuous
water of their own element:

how I remember those women
sweeping in the childish rivers
of my eyes

10   and the fish slipping like
eels through their laughing thighs

Praise Song for My Mother

You were
water to me
deep and bold and fathoming

You were
moon's eye to me
pull and grained and mantling

You were
sunrise to me
rise and warm and streaming

10   You were
the fishes red gill to me
the flame tree's spread to me
the crab's leg/the fried plantain smell
                replenishing replenishing

Go to your wide futures, you said

Iguana Memory

Saw an iguana once
when I was very small
in our backdam backyard
came rustling across my path

green like moving newleaf sunlight

big like big big lizard
with more legs than centipede
so it seemed to me
and it must have stopped a while
10 eyes meeting mine
iguana and child locked in a brief
split moment happening
before it went hurrying

        for the green of its life

Waiting for Thelma's Laughter

(for Thelma, my West Indian born Afro-American neighbour)

You wanna take the world
in hand
and fix-it-up
the way you fix your living room

You wanna reach out and crush
life's big and small injustices
in the fire and honey
of your hands

You wanna scream
10   cause your head's too small
for your dreams

and the children
          running round
            acting like lil clowns
              breaking the furniture down

while I sit through
it all watching you
knowing any time now
your laughter's gonna come

20   to drown and heal us all

Fleur Adcock

The Poet's Introduction

Almost as soon as I could write I began writing poems: I composed my first little verses when I was six, living away from home for a few months during the war. I had a rather mobile childhood: I was born in New Zealand, came to England in 1939, aged five, and returned to New Zealand in 1947. (I now live in London.) During those early years in England I went to eleven schools, for various reasons to do with the war and my father's work. Many years later I decided to write a series of poems about those schools and how it felt to be constantly turning up somewhere as a new girl. (Being an outsider is actually a useful thing for a writer. It sharpens the powers of observation: my younger sister, who had much the same experience, is now a novelist.)

Loving Hitler refers to that time when I was 'unofficially evacuated' to Leicestershire, aged six. It's an attempt to see a minor act of rebellion through the eyes of a child: it uses rather childish language and the device of repetition, which small children enjoy. *Outwood* is another child's eye view, of a place where I lived at seven. I still possess the little notebook I used to write my poems in, illustrated with gawky fairies in elaborate dresses and starry crowns. Writing was partly a way of escaping into a fantasy world and avoiding the rough boys who used to bully me. After Outwood I went to Earlswood where I spent three years, the longest at any school.

Nature Table is also about school-children, but is purely imaginary. What interested me was the differences between people's personalities and preoccupations, even when they're quite young, but the poem also celebrates some of the things I'm fond of – such as tadpoles, which crop up again in the poem of that name, where they form a parallel to the prenatal development of my grandson.

For Heidi with Blue Hair is based on a real incident in the life of my god-daughter Heidi. It's set in Australia, to which she and her father moved after her mother died when Heidi was in her teens. With *The Telephone Call* we come back to fiction, but with a serious point: the poem illustrates the way Fate gets you all excited about something

53

and then kicks you in the teeth. If you read it carefully, though, you'll see that the voice on the telephone doesn't tell any actual lies – it just gives extremely misleading hints: not 'The prize is a million pounds', but 'What would you do with a million pounds?'

I've begun to write more about death now that I'm at an age when some of my friends have died: Heidi's mother, for example, and Pete Laver, in whose memory I wrote *The Keepsake*. Pete had a great sense of humour, and after he died it seemed appropriate to write a poem with jokes in it – his own jokes, the silly quotations he'd enjoyed reading out from the old book he gave me.

These deaths made me even more anxious about the future deaths of my parents. *The Chiffonier* (pronounced to rhyme with 'engineer', not as in French) is based on this fear – and on my mother's habit, shared by many mothers, of mentally dividing up her possessions in advance. I wrote this in rhymed couplets, because that form somehow made it easier to make emotional statements without sounding too heavy. I think of rhyme as a component of light verse, on the whole – as in *The Prize-winning Poem*, which is a piece of light-hearted advice about what to avoid if you want to win a poetry competition (written after I'd judged one which involved reading over 3,000 poems). Rhyme is also appropriate for songs, or anything to be set to music (such as opera). *Street Song* was intended as an actual song, but it also has connections with nursery rhymes, which the names of the streets in Newcastle-upon-Tyne reminded me of. However, it's a sinister nursery-rhyme: the bogeyman figure is that of the 'Yorkshire Ripper' who was thought to be stalking the streets in 1979, when I wrote this. *Witnesses* is another poem about male violence and the difficulties of being a woman in a man's world.

Finally *Last Song*, one of those post-nuclear, end-of-the-world poems that sometimes insist on being written. The idea for this one came to me in bed one night when I was trying to get to sleep: sleepiness and the poem competed for my consciousness, and the poem won.

Loving Hitler

There they were around the wireless
waiting to listen to Lord Haw-Haw.
'Quiet now, children!' they said as usual:
'Ssh, be quiet! We're trying to listen.'
'Germany calling!' said Lord Haw-Haw.

I came out with it: 'I love Hitler.'
They turned on me: 'You can't love *Hitler*!
Dreadful, wicked – ' (mutter, mutter,
the shocked voices buzzing together) –
10   'Don't be silly. You don't mean it.'

I held out for perhaps five minutes,
a mini-proto-neo-Nazi,
six years old and wanting attention.
Hitler always got their attention;
now I had it, for five minutes.

Everyone at school loved someone,
and it had to be a boy or a man
if you were a girl. So why not Hitler?
Of course, you couldn't love Lord Haw-Haw;
20   but Hitler – well, he was so famous!

It might be easier to love Albert,
the boy who came to help with the milking,
but Albert laughed at me. Hitler wouldn't:
one thing you could say for Hitler,
you never heard him laugh at people.

All the same, I settled for Albert.

Outwood

Milkmaids, buttercups, ox-eye daisies,
white and yellow in the tall grass:
I fought my way to school through flowers –
bird's-foot trefoil, clover, vetch –
my sandals all smudged with pollen,
seedy grass-heads caught in my socks.

At school I used to read, mostly,
and hide in the shed at dinnertime,
writing poems in my notebook.
10 'Little fairies dancing', I wrote,
and 'Peter and I, we watch the birds fly,
high in the sky, in the evening.'

Then home across the warm common
to tease my little sister again:
'I suppose you thought I'd been to school:
I've been to work in a bicycle shop.'
Mummy went to a real job
every day, on a real bicycle;

Doris used to look after us.
20 She took us for a walk with a soldier,
through the damp ferns in the wood
into a clearing like a garden,
rosy-pink with beds of campion,
herb-robert, lady's smock.

The blackberry briars were pale with blossom.
I snagged my tussore dress on a thorn;
Doris didn't even notice.
She and the soldier lay on the grass;
he leaned over her pink blouse
30 and their voices went soft and round, like petals.

Earlswood

Air-raid shelters at school were damp tunnels
where you sang 'Ten Green Bottles' yet again
and might as well have been doing decimals.

At home, though, it was cosier and more fun:
cocoa and toast inside the Table Shelter,
our iron-panelled bunker, our new den.

By day we ate off it; at night you'd find us
under it, the floor plump with mattresses
and the wire grilles neatly latched around us.

10   You had to be careful not to bump your head;
we padded the hard metal bits with pillows,
then giggled in our glorious social bed.

What could be safer? What could be more romantic
than playing cards by torchlight in a raid?
Odd that it made our mother so neurotic

to hear the sirens; we were quite content –
but slightly cramped once there were four of us,
after we'd taken in old Mrs Brent

from down by the Nag's Head, who'd been bombed out.
20   She had her arm in plaster, but she managed
to dress herself, and smiled, and seemed all right.

Perhaps I just imagined hearing her
moaning a little in the night, and shaking
splinters of glass out of her long grey hair.

The next week we were sent to Leicestershire.

Nature Table

The tadpoles won't keep still in the aquarium;
Ben's tried seven times to count them –
thirty-two, thirty-three, wriggle, wriggle –
all right, he's got better things to do.

Heidi stares into the tank, wearing
a snail on her knuckle like a ring.
She can see purple clouds in the water,
a sky for the tadpoles in their world.

Matthew's drawing a worm. Yesterday
10 he put one down Elizabeth's neck.
But these are safely locked in the wormery
eating their mud; he's tried that too.

Laura sways with her nose in a daffodil,
drunk on pollen, her eyes tight shut.
The whole inside of her head is filling
with a slow hum of fizzy yellow.

Tom squashes his nose against the window.
He hopes it may look like a snail's belly
to the thrush outside. But is not attacked:
20 the thrush is happy on the bird-table.

The wind ruffles a chaffinch's crest
and gives the sparrows frilly grey knickers
as they squabble over their seeds and bread.
The sun swings in and out of clouds.

Ben's constructing a wigwam of leaves
for the snails. Heidi whispers to the tadpoles
'Promise you won't start eating each other!'
Matthew's rather hoping they will.

A wash of sun sluices the window,
30 bleaches Tom's hair blonder, separates
Laura from her daffodil with a sneeze,
and sends the tadpoles briefly frantic;

until the clouds flop down again
grey as wet canvas. The wind quickens,
birds go flying, window-glass rattles,
pellets of hail are among the birdseed.

Tadpoles

For Oliver

Their little black thread legs, their threads of arms,
their mini-miniature shoulders, elbows, knees –
this piquant angularity, delicious
after that rippling smoothness, after nothing
but a flow of curves and roundnesses in water;
and their little hands, the size of their hands, the fingers
like hair-stubble, and their clumps-of-eyelashes feet...

Taddies, accept me as your grandmother,
a hugely gloating grand-maternal frog,
10 almost as entranced by other people's
tadpoles as I once was by my own,
that year when Oliver was still a tadpole
in Elizabeth's womb, and I a grandmother
only prospectively, and at long distance.

All this glory from globes of slithery glup!
Well, slithery glup was all right, with its cloudy
compacted spheres, its polka dots of blackness.
Then dots evolved into commas; the commas hatched.
When they were nothing but animated match-heads
20   with tails, a flickering flock of magnified
spermatazoa, they were already my darlings.

And Oliver lay lodged in his dreamy sphere,
a pink tadpole, a promise of limbs and language,
while my avatars of infancy grew up
into ribbon-tailed black-currants, fluttery-smooth,
and then into soaked brown raisins, a little venous,
with touches of transparency at the sides
where limbs minutely hinted at themselves.

It is the transformation that enchants.
30   As a mother reads her child's form in the womb,
imaging eyes and fingers, radar-sensing
a thumb in a blind mouth, so tadpole-watchers
can stare at the cunning shapes beneath the skin
and await the tiny, magnificent effloration.
It is a lesson for a grandmother.

My tadpoles grew to frogs in their generation;
they may have been the grandparents of these
about-to-be frogs. And Oliver's a boy,
hopping and bouncing in his bright green tracksuit,
40   my true darling; but too far away now
for me to call him across the world and say
'Oliver, look at what's happening to the tadpoles!'

For Heidi with Blue Hair

When you dyed your hair blue
(or, at least, ultramarine
for the clipped sides, with a crest
of jet-black spikes on top)
you were sent home from school

because, as the headmistress put it,
although dyed hair was not
specifically forbidden, yours
was, apart from anything else,
10   not done in the school colours.

Tears in the kitchen, telephone-calls
to school from your freedom-loving father:
'She's not a punk in her behaviour;
it's just a style.' (You wiped your eyes,
also not in a school colour.)

'She discussed it with me first –
we checked the rules.' 'And anyway, Dad,
it cost twenty-five dollars.
Tell them it won't wash out –
20   not even if I wanted to try.'

It would have been unfair to mention
your mother's death, but that
shimmered behind the arguments.
The school had nothing else against you;
the teachers twittered and gave in.

Next day your black friend had hers done
in grey, white and flaxen yellow –
the school colours precisely:
an act of solidarity, a witty
30   tease. The battle was already won.

The Telephone Call

They asked me 'Are you sitting down?
Right? This is Universal Lotteries',
they said. 'You've won the top prize,
the Ultra-super Global Special.
What would you do with a million pounds?
Or, actually, with more than a million –
not that it makes a lot of difference
once you're a millionaire.' And they laughed.

'Are you OK?' they asked – 'Still there?
10 Come on, now, tell us, how does it feel?'
I said 'I just... I can't believe it!'
They said 'That's what they all say.
What else? Go on, tell us about it.'
I said 'I feel the top of my head
has floated off, out through the window,
revolving like a flying saucer.'

'That's unusual' they said. 'Go on.'
I said 'I'm finding it hard to talk.
My throat's gone dry, my nose is tingling.
20 I think I'm going to sneeze – or cry.'
'That's right' they said, 'don't be ashamed
of giving way to your emotions.
It isn't every day you hear
you're going to get a million pounds.

Relax, now, have a little cry;
we'll give you a moment... ' 'Hang on!' I said.
'I haven't bought a lottery ticket
for years and years. And what did you say
the company's called?' They laughed again.
30 'Not to worry about a ticket.

We're Universal. We operate
A retrospective Chances Module.

Nearly everyone's bought a ticket
in some lottery or another,
once at least. We buy up the files,
feed the names into our computer,
and see who the lucky person is.'
'Well, that's incredible' I said.
'It's marvellous. I still can't quite…
40 I'll believe it when I see the cheque.'

'Oh,' they said, 'there's no cheque.'
'But the money?' 'We don't deal in money.
Experiences are what we deal in.
You've had a great experience, right?
Exciting? Something you'll remember?
That's your prize. So congratulations
from all of us at Universal.
Have a nice day!' And the line went dead.

The Chiffonier

You're glad I like the chiffonier. But I
feel suddenly uneasy, scenting why
you're pleased I like this pretty thing you've bought,
the twin of one that stood beside your cot
when you were small: you've marked it down for me;
it's not too heavy to be sent by sea
when the time comes, and it's got space inside
to pack some other things you've set aside,
things that are small enough to go by water
10   twelve thousand miles to me, your English daughter.
I know your habits – writing all our names
in books and on the backs of picture-frames,
allotting antique glass and porcelain dishes
to granddaughters according to their wishes,
promising me the tinted photograph
of my great-grandmother. We used to laugh,
seeing how each occasional acquisition
was less for you than for later disposition:
'You know how Marilyn likes blue and white
20   china? I've seen some plates I thought I might
indulge in.' Bless you, Mother! But we're not
quite so inclined to laugh now that you've got
something that's new to you but not a part
of your estate: that weakness in your heart.
It makes my distance from you, when I go
back home next week, suddenly swell and grow
from thirty hours' flying to a vast
galactic space between present and past.
How many more times can I hope to come
30   to Wellington and find you still at home?
We've talked about it, as one has to, trying
to see the lighter aspects of your dying:

'You've got another twenty years or more'
I said, 'but when you think you're at death's door
just let me know. I'll come and hang about
for however long it takes to see you out.'
'I don't think it'll be like that' you said:
'I'll pop off suddenly one night in bed.'

How secretive! How satisfying! You'll
40 sneak off, a kid running away from school –
well, that at least's the only way I find
I can bring myself to see it in my mind.
But now I see you in your Indian skirt
and casual cornflower-blue linen shirt
in the garden, under your feijoa tree,
looking about as old or young as me.
Dear little Mother! Naturally I'm glad
you found a piece of furniture that had
happy associations with your youth;
50 and yes, I do admire it – that's the truth:
its polished wood and touch of Art Nouveau
appeal to me. But surely you must know
I value this or any other treasure
of yours chiefly because it gives you pleasure.
I have to write this now, while you're still here:
I want my mother, not her chiffonier.

The Keepsake

In memory of Pete Laver

'To Fleur from Pete, on loan perpetual.'
It's written on the flyleaf of the book
I wouldn't let you give away outright:
'Just make it permanent loan' I said – a joke
between librarians, professional
jargon. It seemed quite witty, on a night

when most things passed for wit. We were all hoarse
by then, from laughing at the bits you'd read
aloud – the heaving bosoms, blushing sighs,
10   demoniac lips. 'Listen to this!' you said:
' "Thus rendered bold by frequent intercourse
I dared to take her hand". ' We wiped our eyes.

' "Colonel, what mean these stains upon your dress?" '
We howled. And then there was Lord Ravenstone
faced with Augusta's dutiful rejection
in anguished prose; or, for a change of tone,
a touch of Gothic: Madame la Comtesse
's walled-up lover. An inspired collection:

The Keepsake, 1835; the standard
20   drawing-room annual, useful as a means
for luring ladies into chaste flirtation
in early 19th century courtship scenes.
I'd never seen a copy; often wondered.
Well, here it was – a pretty compilation

of tales and verses: stanzas by Lord Blank
and Countess This and Mrs That; demure
engravings, all white shoulders, corkscrew hair
and swelling bosoms; stories full of pure
sentiments, in which gentlemen of rank
30 urged suits upon the nobly-minded fair.

You passed the volume round, and poured more wine.
Outside your cottage lightning flashed again:
A Grasmere storm, theatrically right
for stories of romance and terror. Then
somehow, quite suddenly, the book was mine.
The date in it's five weeks ago tonight.

'On loan perpetual.' If that implied
some dark finality, some hint of *nox
perpetua*, something desolate and bleak,
40 we didn't see it then, among the jokes.
Yesterday, walking on the fells, you died.
I'm left with this, a trifling, quaint antique.

You'll not reclaim it now; it's mine to keep:
a keepsake, nothing more. You've changed the 'loan
perpetual' to a bequest by dying.
Augusta, Lady Blanche, Lord Ravenstone –
I've read the lot, trying to get to sleep.
The jokes have all gone flat. I can't stop crying.

The Prize-winning Poem

It will be typed, of course, and not all in capitals: it will
    use upper and lower case
in the normal way; and where a space is usual it will have
    a space.
It will probably be on white paper, or possibly blue, but
    almost certainly not pink.
It will not be decorated with ornamental scroll-work in
    coloured ink,
nor will a photograph of the poet be glued above his or her
    name,
and still less a snap of the poet's children frolicking in a
    jolly game.
The poem will not be about feeling lonely and being fifteen
and unless the occasion of the competition is a royal jubilee it
    will not be about the queen.
It will not be the first poem the author has written in his
    life
10   and will probably not be about the death of his daughter,
    son or wife
because although to write such elegies fulfils a therapeutic
    need
in large numbers they are deeply depressing for the judges
    to read.
The title will not be 'Thoughts' or 'Life' or 'I Wonder
    Why'
or 'The Bunny-rabbit's Birthday Party' or 'In Days of
    Long Gone By'.
'Tis and 'twas, o'er and e'er, and such poetical
    contractions will not be found
in the chosen poem. Similarly clichés will not abound:
dawn will not herald another bright new day, nor dew
    sparkle like diamonds in a dell,

nor trees their arms upstretch. Also the poet will be able
to spell.
Large meaningless concepts will not be viewed with
favour: myriad is out;
20 infinity is becoming suspect; aeons and galaxies are in
some doubt.
Archaisms and inversions will not occur; nymphs will not
their fate bemoan.
Apart from this there will be no restrictions upon the style
or tone.
What is required is simply the masterpiece we'd all write
if we could.
There is only one prescription for it: it's got to be good.

Street Song

Pink Lane, Strawberry Lane, Pudding Chare:
someone is waiting, I don't know where;
hiding among the nursery names,
he wants to play peculiar games.

In Leazes Terrace or Leazes Park
someone is loitering in the dark,
feeling the giggles rise in his throat
and fingering something under his coat.

He could be sidling along Forth Lane
10   to stop some girl from catching her train,
or stalking the grounds of the RVI
to see if a student nurse goes by.

In Belle Grove Terrace or Fountain Row
or Hunter's Road he's raring to go –
unless he's the quiet shape you'll meet
on the cobbles in Back Stowell Street.

Monk Street, Friars Street, Gallowgate
are better avoided when it's late.
Even in Sandhill and the Side
20   there are shadows where a man could hide.

So don't go lightly along Darn Crook
because the Ripper's been brought to book.
Wear flat shoes, and be ready to run:
remember, sisters, there's more than one.

Witnesses

We three in our dark decent clothes,
unlike ourselves, more like the three
witches, we say, crouched over the only
ashtray, smoke floating into our hair,

wait. An hour; another hour.
If you stand up and walk ten steps
to the glass doors you can see her there
in the witness box, a Joan of Arc,

10   straight, still, her neck slender,
her lips moving from time to time
in reply to voices we can't hear:
'I put it to you… I should like to suggest… '

It's her small child who is at stake.
His future hangs from these black-clad
proceedings, these ferretings under her sober
dress, under our skirts and dresses

to sniff out corruption: 'I put it to you
that in fact your husband… that my client…
that you yourself initiated the violence…
20   that your hysteria… ' She sits like marble.

We pace the corridors, peep at the distance
from door to witness box (two steps up,
remember, be careful not to trip
when the time comes) and imagine them there,

the ones we can't see. A man in a wig
and black robes. Two other men
in lesser wigs and gowns. More men
in dark suits. We sit down together,

shake the smoke from our hair, pass round
30   more cigarettes (to be held carefully
so as not to smirch our own meek versions
of their clothing), and wait to be called.

Last Song

Goodbye, sweet symmetry. Goodbye, sweet world
of mirror-images and matching halves,
where animals have usually four legs
and people nearly always two;
where birds and bats and butterflies and bees
have balanced wings, and even flies
can fly straight if they try. Goodbye
to one-a-side for eyes and ears and arms
and breasts and balls and shoulder-blades
10   and hands; goodbye to the straight line
drawn down the central spine,
making us double in a world
where oddness is acceptable only
under the sea, for the lop-sided lobster,
the wonky oyster, the creepily rotated
flatfish with both eyes over one gill;
goodbye to the sweet certitudes of our
mammalian order, where to be
born with one eye or three thumbs
20   points to not being human. It will come.

In the next world, when this one's gone skew-wiff,
we shall be algae or lichen, things
we've hardly even needed to pronounce.
If the flounder still exists it will be king.

Carol Rumens

The Poet's Introduction

I began to write stories and poems as soon as I could write, and long before I could spell properly. I was an only child from a lower middle-class background: we lived in a flat in my grandparents' house in Forest Hill, South London. Because I wasn't allowed to play on, or even cross, the main road outside, I was given plenty of crayons, pencils and paper to keep me quiet and amused indoors. I loved drawing and painting as well, and always illustrated my 'books', as I used to call the three-penny note-pads in which I wrote.

I was fortunate, I think, in being sent to a Catholic school, despite the fact that we weren't Catholics and I always felt an outsider. (What did 'Protestant' mean? What I was protesting about I couldn't imagine!) My life was filled with hymns and prayers and rituals, and I responded powerfully to the magic of the long, rhythmical words, especially, perhaps, when I didn't understand them. Bad words (the ones I mustn't say at home) and frightening words (such as those in my grandma's medical book) exercised a more horrible fascination.

I wrote *At Puberty* in my mid-twenties, but I think it captures some of the atmosphere of my later schooldays. Its setting is the grammar school to which I won a scholarship, a state school administered by nuns (the 'dark blue brides of Christ') but employing a number of lay women teachers. At 13, I fell in love with one of those teachers, and with music at the same time, especially Mozart's. My feelings were intense and wonderful, yet also somehow hopeless. Though by the time I wrote the poem I was married and had two small daughers of my own, I was still able to summon up the experience from my memory as if it had just happened. Imaginative time is not linear; it consists of layers, and one of the thrills of writing is to be able to dive down into those layers and find life!

I rarely write poems simply about landscape or visual phenomena: though I do not consider myself a very sociable person, when I write I seem to recover a buried interest in people. However, I think it is

73

the inaccessible characters that fascinate me most. I have written a number of poems about my father since his death. *December Walk* is about our relationship during his last illness. *A Dream of South Africa* tries, partly, to come to terms with the fact that, as a shipper, he had worked for a company with contacts with the South African government, of which I strongly disapproved. At the same time he was the kindest of men, and, I think, secretly disillusioned. He had wanted to travel the world, and that was why he became a shipper.

I like to write both free and formal poetry. Of course, many people think that 'free verse' is the lazy way out for modern poets, but in fact it's very much harder than formal verse to write well; you are thrown back on your own instincts for phrasing and shaping, just as you are when you write a story or a novel. Every poem must have a form, even if it is one that you let your material evolve as it goes along: T. S. Eliot was quite right in saying that there is really no such thing as 'vers libre'.

Two examples of my formal verse are *Rules for Beginners*, which is a sestina, and *Ballad of the Morning After*. In both these poems I was doing something which might be called 'pouring new wine into old bottles', that is, using a contemporary diction and consciousness within an ancient, or traditional, structure. In the case of the sestina, the consciousness is that of a working-class girl of the 1960s, in the ballad, it is that of a would-be liberated woman of the 1980s, painfully involved in an extra-marital affair.

I called my second book *Unplayed Music* because, growing up, I had finally abandoned my hopes of becoming a professional musician and had resolved to put all my creative energies into writing. The title poem of that collection is again about a relationship that is unfulfilled – this time because it is in its very early stages. Poems like this accept the ordinary limitations on human relationships. They are not revolutionary or challenging, but I hope they are honest.

Occasionally I'll tackle a more obviously political theme. I think political poetry is hard to write well; like love poetry it draws on emotions so deep you can drown in them. If you start writing a poem with a lot of strong opinions in your head, however admirable and 'right on' these are, they can make the poem sound too 'easy' and even rather false. *Two Women* is a poem that shines a fairly bright 'political' light on an area of personal experience. I see late twentieth-century England as an increasingly harsh and ungenerous society. I doubt that poetry by itself can effect big political changes, but I think it helps in its gently subversive way to increase the power of opposition. Poetry may be a miniaturist art, at least in comparison with the mass media, but it is far from trivial; it keeps us in touch with the details of being human and makes discoveries about emotional truths that are at least as important to us as the physical discoveries of science.

At Puberty

After rain
a blue light settled over the convent arches.

The naked asphalt astonished itself with diamonds.
Even the exhausted plaster virgin
in the Bernadette Grotto and the mulberry tree,
propped up, and barren of silkworms,
stepped cleanly out of their decay.

From the back of the music lesson,
a girl stared through a window,
10   watching beam upon beam of realisation
incise the long mist of her childhood.

Komm liebe Mai
sang the class, uneasily.
A new emotion,
innocent, classical,
yet making her blush and burn
was softly unravelled
by the clear-eyed woman who sat
at the black Bösendorfer
20   with her coquettishness and her merciless,
gentle arpeggios.

The elm-leaves turned, silver-backed,
on a wind coarse as hunger.

And nuns in their distant sanctuary,
the dark-blue brides of Christ,
closed their ears to the sin, the soft,
tired alto of girls at puberty;
heard still a child's soprano.

O impossible miracles, light
30   out of straggle-rowed chairs
and school-room floorboards!

The girl, pale as clouds,
stares for a year

at the vision which cannot see
the speechless peasant,

which will suddenly vanish, leaving
only an enormous grief
like a deep river between them

– the woman who needed nothing
40   and the child who promised everything.

The Advanced Set

My three mysterious uncles
were my father's elder brothers,
but not like him at all.

Arranged in steps, by age,
their three small portraits frowned
above the tea-time doilies.

They didn't frown at me,
but as if they sensed
each other's eyes, too close.

10   My grandma, sawing bread,
glanced back at them before telling
how they took care not to speak

when, by an oversight,
they were in the house together.
They ate in relays.

What did they do next?
They went to war. One
got taken prisoner.

(His tortured shadow lurked
20   dark-yellowish in the damp-stain
behind the print of Mount Fuji.)

One lived by the sea.
He had asthma and a mistress.
The other drank port-wine,

alone and grand in Tonbridge,
officer-class to the end.
Without a word they slipped

past my childhood gaze,
having never patted my head
30   or spun me a sixpence.

Those three Advanced Level uncles
– complex as love affairs,
far as the Burma Road –

might have talked to me in the end
but had the wit to die
before I grew tall enough

to sweep the brown photos down,
laugh at them, dance on them,
sigh, 'But you're ordinary.'

A Dream of South Africa

Trafalgar Square is only a pigeon-sea,
but he could hear the waves sigh up and fall
as he passed the sooty door-stones of Pall Mall.
The men in their navy suits were sailors, he
a brisk cadet. He marched behind, in step,
towards the lighted windows of his ship.

An office job! It didn't seem like work,
So I painted it in childish, Admiral colours.
My mother laughed, fought off the social climbers…
10   In fact, he was a ship-broker's clerk,
the fourth, last, disappointing son,
sea-feverish since the age of seventeen.

Cathay Pacific, Cunard, Peninsular House
– one night not long ago I followed him
– saw where he boozed – the Travellers', the Reform.
The wind hustled his stumpy, pin-striped ghost,
practised now, and as managerial,
almost, as if he'd been an admiral.

He stayed becalmed in these local pools,
20   drawn by the whisky siren's easy mood.
'South Africa,' she whispered, and he glowed,
imagining that palm-green, palm-court cruise,
a charming old imperialist of the fleet,
who'd crunch the diamonds under hard, white feet.

If he had doubts, he didn't ever say,
although he sometimes talked about retirement.
Once, he brought home from the Embassy
a pamphlet – boring, but it sounded decent.
It offered 'separate development for the Bantu'.
30   'Apartheid' tripped my tongue; a long word, new.

I've never understood what happened later.
My mother grumbled no directorship,
no retirement cruise, no Africa.
Age moves so fast, the young just can't keep up...
The liners that slid, shining, down the Thames
had sailed without him. Or he'd sailed without them.

Cathay Pacific, Cunard, Peninsular House:
I listed them, as he must have done
with boyish love, before he veered off-course
40   – wrong man, wrong job – but kept his head down,
having a wife and daughter to support,
until the lights went out on his horizon.

Over the Bridge

Cowboys, free-rangers of the late-night bus routes,
they hit the town again, sucked cigarettes
fizzing as they lean into the edges
of corners, talk in nudges
and jeers – three ten-year-olds, too tough
for girls, though girls they'll brag of, soon enough,
their long, pale hair brokenly raked
beyond the line of last month's makeshift
barbering, frayed shirtcuffs falling short
10   to flash expensive watches, newly bought.

The city's greased and rapid
machinery is their passion; they'll work it
to the last cog, discovering all the loopholes
– how to tilt the pintables
and not lose the game, when to slip
their pocketful and saunter from the shop.

School can't detain them; they've cut the nets
of that soft playground. The lesson drifts
above their empty desks like a will read
20   solemnly to the disinherited.

Westminster Bridge veers up. They clatter down,
jump for its back, are straggling shadows, blown
and tiny as they run to see themselves
V-signing back from windows of black waves.
Further and further now from the controls,
they wander out of history, though its spires
rise in gold above them. The clock's proud face
makes no comment, shines on some other place.

One Street Beyond

From first light to pub time,
always the trackless children
skirmishing, sliding
through the grit of empty underpasses;
making a chase-game,
throwing coke-cans, threats,
tumbling down the absurd
grass flanks of the main road.
All day you hear them,
10   tractors and go-carts squealing
in mindless circles.
All day, some are clambering,
stranded on one
rusting climbing-frame.
Some are running away,
and others, standing staring
at a vacant play-space.

All through the long August
they are darkening, hardening
20 – the outdoor children
whose fathers come and leave
in vans or on foot
without a word;
whose mothers are always tired
and shouting from windows.
Making little, barbed worlds
from broken glass and match-sticks
at the edges of kerbs,
the children never listen.
30 They started with white socks,
new toys, washed faces,
but always end here,
dirty and alone,
one street beyond
justice or love.

Rules for Beginners

They said: 'Honour thy father and thy mother.
Don't spend every evening at the Disco.
Listen to your teachers, take an O level
or two. Of course, one day you'll have children.
We've tried our best to make everything nice.
Now it's up to you to be an adult!'

She went to all the 'X' films like an adult.
Sometimes she hung around the Mecca Disco.
Most of the boys she met were dead O level,
10 smoking and swearing, really great big children.
She had a lot of hassle with her mother;
it was always her clothes or her friends that weren't nice.

At school some of the teachers were quite nice,
but most of them thought they were minding children.
'Now Susan,' they would say, 'You're nearly adult
– behave like one!' The snobs taking O level
never had fun, never went to the Disco;
they did their homework during 'Listen with Mother'.

She said: 'I'd hate to end up like my mother,
20 but there's this lovely bloke down at the Disco
who makes me feel a lot more like an adult.
He murmured – 'When I look at you, it's nice
all over! Can't you cut that old O level
scene? Christ, I could give you twenty children!'

He had to marry her. There were three children
– all girls. Sometimes she took them to her mother
to get a break. She tried to keep them nice.
It was dull all day with kids, the only adult.
She wished they'd told you that, instead of O level.
30 Sometimes she dragged her husband to the Disco.

She got a part-time job at the Disco,
behind the bar; a neighbour had the children.
Now she knew all about being an adult
and honestly it wasn't very nice.
Her husband grumbled – 'Where's the dinner, mother?'
'I'm going down the night-school for an O level,

I am,' said mother. 'Have fun at the Disco,
kids! When you're an adult, life's all O level.
Stay clear of children, keep your figures nice!'

Two Women

Daily to a profession – paid thinking
and clean hands – she rises,
unquestioning. It's second nature now.
The hours, though they're all of daylight, suit her.
The desk, typewriter, carpets, pleasantries
are a kind of civilization – built on money
of course, but money, now she sees, is human.
She has learned giving from a bright new chequebook,
intimacy from absence. Coming home
10   long after dark to the jugular torrent
of family life, she brings,
tucked in her bag, the simple, cool-skinned apples
of a father's loving objectivity.
That's half the story. There's another woman
who bears her name, a silent, background face
that's always flushed with work, or swallowed anger.
A true wife, she picks up scattered laundry
and sets the table with warmed plates to feed
the clean-handed woman. They've not met.
20   If they were made to touch, they'd burn each other.

Ballad of the Morning After

Take back the festive midnight
Take back the sad-eyed dawn
Wind up that old work ethic
Oh let me be unborn.

After a night of travelling
How can it come to pass
That there's the same tongue in my mouth
The same face in my glass

Same light on the curtain
10   Same thirst in the cup
Same ridiculous notion
Of never getting up?

Cars stream above the city
The subway throbs below
Whirling a million faces
Like shapeless scraps of snow

And all these melting faces
Flying below and above
Think they are loved especially
20   Think they especially love

This is a free country
The jails are for the bad
The only British dissidents
Are either poor or mad.

I put my classless jeans on
Open my lockless door
I breathe the air of freedom
And know I'm mad and poor.

Love is the creed I grew by
30   Love is the liberal's drug
Not Agape but Eros
With his Utopian hug

And in the *close, supportive*
Environment of the bed,
He is liberty, equality,
Fraternity and bread.

That is the supposition
But I say love's a joke
A here-today-and-gone-tomorrow
40   Childish pinch-and-poke.

Perhaps I'll believe in something
Like God or Politics
I'd build those temples wider
But there are no more bricks.

Some women believe in Sisterhood
They've rowed the Master's ship
Across the lustful silver sea
On his last ego-trip.

And some believe in Housework,
50   And a few believe in Men.
There's only one man that I want,
And I want him again and again.

He sat down at my table.
He finished all the wine.
'You're nothing, dear, to me,' he said,
But his body covered mine,

And stoked the fiery sickness
That's done me to a turn

– The fool that chose to marry
60   And also chose to burn.

Burning burning burning
I came to self-abuse,
Hoping I'd go blind, but no,
It wasn't any use.

I see a mother and her child
Both turn with starving face.
And that's the story of our lives,
The whole damned human race.

My conscience is a hangover,
70   My sex-life, chemistry;
My values are statistics,
My opinions, PMT.

Beside my rented window
I listen to the rain.
Yes, love's a ball of iron,
And time its short, sharp chain.

The middle-aged say life's too short.
The old and young say 'wrong'.
I'll tell you, if you don't like life,
80   It's every day too long.

Gifts and Loans

They meet in the mornings over coffee,
their only bond, work, and being married
to other people. They begin with jokes
– the chairman, the weather, the awful journey –
delicately pacing out their common ground.

Later, they expand into description.
Families, who might not recognize themselves,
are called up in brisk bulletins,
edited for maximum entertainment.
10 (Gossip ignores their middle-aged laughter.)

She shows him a photo of her sons,
tanned and smiling over fishing-nets
one green June day when the light was perfect.
He talks about his daughters, both away
at college. They admire everything.

Through the months more curious, more honest,
they cultivate small permissions, remember
each other in the fading summer evenings,
and suddenly get up from their lives,
20 to hunt for a book, or pick some fruit.

No quarrels cloud the simple space between them.
They imagine how their adequate weekends
might shimmer with this other happiness
– and how, perhaps, they'd still end up with less
than haunts a gift of pears, a borrowed book.

A Marriage

Mondays, he trails burr-like fragments
of the weekend to London
    a bag of soft, yellow apples from his trees
    a sense of being loved and laundered.

He shows me a picture of marriage
as a whole, small civilization,
its cities, rosewood and broadloom,
its religion, the love of children

whose anger it survived
10 long ago, and who now return like lambs,
disarmed, adoring.
His wife sits by the window,

one hand planting tapestry daisies.
She smiles as he offers her the perfect apple.
On its polished, scented skin
falls a Renaissance gilding.

These two have kept their places,
trusting the old rules
of decorous counterpoint.
20 Now their lives are rich with echoes.

Later, she'll carry a boxful
of apples to school. Her six-year-olds
will weigh, then eat, them, thrilling
to a flavour sharp as tears.

I listen while he tells me about her sewing,
as if I were the square of dull cloth
and his voice the leaping needle
chasing its tail in a dazzle of wonderment.

He places an apple in my hand;
30   then, for a moment, I must become his child.
To look at him as a woman
would turn me cold with shame.

Unplayed Music

We stand apart in the crowd that slaps its filled glasses
on the green piano, quivering her shut heart.
The tavern, hung with bottles, winks and sways
like a little ship, smuggling its soul through darkness.
There is an arm flung jokily round my shoulders,
and clouds of words and smoke thicken between us.
I watch you watching me. All else is blindness.

Outside, the long street glimmers pearl.
Our revellers' heat steams into the cold
10   as fresh snow, crisping and slithering
underfoot, witches us back to childhood.
Oh night of ice and Schnapps, moonshine and stars,
how lightly two of us have fallen in step
behind the crowd! The shadowy white landscape
gathers our few words into its secret.

All night in the small grey room
I'm listening for you, for the new music
waiting only to be played; all night I hear nothing
but wind over the snow, my own heart beating.

Days and Nights

It's a summer day very nearly like any other.
The pollen count rises in the afternoon.
An Iranian child steals a lemon in Selfridges.
The discontent of the unions rumbles dully
like a pit disaster many miles away,
while, in a murmuring classroom,
a young teacher is telling her six-year-olds
about the miracle of the loaves and fishes.
The first Royal Garden Party is held,
10 and afterwards the small hills of Green Park
stream dark suits, pastel hats, flowing skirts
and the low, excited conversation
of church-goers after an unusual sermon.
Even the tired marquee waitresses,
leaving by the Electrician's Gate
with sprays of left-over rose-buds, feel uplifted.
Two nurses, one on nights,
one, days, swap their only pair of shoes.
Along Park Lane there are lights and dinners,
20 middle-aged lust and young nostalgias.
It's a summer night very nearly like any other.
The traffic thins, the stars keep their distance.
The Chancellor dreams vaguely about the bank-rate.

Tides

The other night I slept in a red-roofed village
that was trying not to topple off the land.
Outside the Seamen's Mission a rusty-scaled
cod gasped for coins, standing tip-tailed,
but I turned in at the sign of the Dolphin, where
the landlord drank like a ghost at his own bar,
and his dog barked 'time' in the small hours.
I escaped at dawn to clear my head with the wind
that bounded out across the turfy clay
10   where at last the moor slipped into the arms of the bay.

Three hundred miles from the pinpoint of a chance
of meeting you, I was perfectly cool.
I watched the sea drag its malevolent, gleaming
tons away from the land it had just darkened,
and was glad I would be cosily south before
it hurtled back to boil at the sea-wall
and unveil a winter, the streets white or streaming,
the mouth of the mission-cod encrusted with ice,
and no one stooping on the pooly sand
20   to weigh the small cold of a starfish in a warm hand.

When I took the little creature from my pocket
later, I found it had changed shape, as if
in some last, inching retreat from life,
it had been reborn. I placed it in a glass,
freshly filled, with some salt from the breakfast table
– but it didn't stir again. I suppose I'd thought
it might unfurl like a Japanese water-flower,
brimmed with its element. So the foolish hope for
resurrection, or at least the kind of death
30   that brightens corn-rot to alcohol, driftwood to jet.

All that remained now was a valediction
to tender doubt, and the backward-racing lines
of the railway, sepia after a night of rain,
since I had to come home, leaving the dead starfish
for the landlady, leaving the village
to its history of cod and non-conformist virtue,
and the helpless plunge of its streets to their salty source,
leaving the chastened tourists clambering still
towards the mysteries of some clouded hill;
40   since I had to trade the rich North sea for stone;
talk with you, touch you, let the tide turn.

December Walk

i.m. W. A. Lumley

1

He can go outside, said the nurse,
and so I eased him
towards the door, and into
the last of the afternoon.
He was like frozen washing,
the arm my hand clutched
a brittle stick
from the garden's silvered blackness,
his complexion, white as a china-doll's,
10   and a pitiful, aged innocence
in his thin smiling.
The dark suit that wasn't his
hung on him.
The faded shirt, buttoned high,
had a crease ironed into it
where the tie should have been.

Clutching a shred of tissue,
he groped the few yards
around the hospital block
20 as if it were stony miles.
I tried to match his tread.
Perhaps he was right
and this was a great journey.
Perhaps a lifetime of hopes
and conclusions was arrayed
along that gravel strip
edging a muddy lawn,
and nothing else was required,
no afterwards.
30 I kissed him goodbye.
He shut his eyes.
Outside the day was still, breath-white
– the shroud he would be sewn in.

2

Pacing behind him,
  I imagine how light he must be.
The bearers' tall, black shoulders
would never admit it.
They are braced for immensity.
The organ takes up the pretence,
40 and the chrysanthemums, trembling
their frilly gold Baroque
through icy chapel air.
In plain pews built
too narrow for kneeling
we remove our gloves
and pray from small books.
He was somebody once,
but sickened, and lost
all the weight of himself.

50 He forgot our names
and wandered for years,
words melting off his back
like snowflakes. I recall
barely a mood, a flickering
of smiled irony,
now as the altar screen
slides on its hidden runner
to blot out doomed wood
discreetly: that,
60 and a willingness, flat and English
as the whited winter sky,
to be always disappointed.
He was an unbeliever
in everything he did.
He would have had a hand
in this, perhaps, approving
our boredom, the sad weather
and what there is of ash.

The Girl in the Cathedral

for Andrew and Joanna

Daring to watch over Martyrs and Archbishops
Stretched in their full-length slumbers, sharp-nosed Deans,
Princes and Knights still dressed for wars as dim
As bronze, slim feet at rest upon the flanks
Of long-unwhistled hounds; daring the chills
And dusts that cling to stiffly soaring branches,
This small eloquence is a stone so plain
It cannot go unread, a chiselled spray
Of drooping buds, a name, a date, an age.
10 Susannah Starr died at ten years old,
And no one knows why her timid presence
Should be commended here. While history filled
The log-books of these lives, she sat apart,
A well-bred child, perhaps, patient with tutors
And needlepoint, perhaps a foundling, saved
By some lean churchman, warming to his duty.
Quietly during 1804
The blind was drawn, the half-stitched sampler folded.
Whoever mourned her must have carried weight
20 And bought her this pale space to ease his grief
As if such sainted company could speed
Her journeying soul, or because he guessed
The power of one short name and 'ten years old'
To strip the clothes from all these emperors,
And rouse her simple ghost, our pointless tears.

Carpet-weavers, Morocco

The children are at the loom of another world.
Their braids are oiled and black, their dresses bright.
Their assorted heights would make a melodious chime.

They watch their flickering knots like television.
As the garden of Islam grows, the bench will be raised.
Then they will lace the dark-rose veins of the tree-tops.

The carpet will travel in the merchant's truck.
It will be spread by the servants of the mosque.
Deep and soft, it will give when heaped with prayer.

10 The children are hard at work in the school of days.
From their fingers the colours of all-that-will-be fly
and freeze into the frame of all-that-was.

Selima Hill

The Poet's Introduction

I think I became a writer because I wanted to have a friend. Both my parents were painters and were much older than anyone else's parents; and our house was tall and dark, and I was lonely.

But, while acknowledging writing as my ally and my friend, I also came to see it as a kind of enemy – a black, shaggy, misshapen animal that lives in my yard, in secret, and won't leave me alone.

Sometimes I wish I was a nice ordinary friendly person without this compulsion to write; and then I tell myself that writing is a good thing because it is a way of sharing and it helps us to be aware of who we are: just the fact of writing about something is a way of celebrating it, of saying 'thank you' to it. In fact, I see each poem as a kind of prayer. I do not want to judge, but to be still and understand.

From my realization of how much writing has helped me as a shy person, to talk about my experiences, and share them with other people, I began to want to encourage other people to write as well, especially those silenced or isolated in some way, such as people who live in hospices or prisons. Let me quote the Polish poet, Czeslaw Milosz: 'Our house is open, there are no keys in the doors and invisible guests come in and out at will...'

All but one of the poems here were written not for publication (they are from my first book), but as a way of thinking about things that had happened to me – they are all autobiographical, as first books usually are – of taking my feelings out, from inside of me, on to the white open page.

My house was always full of animals and children at this time – I was a child minder, as well as having three children of my own. I planned the poems when I was out with the dogs and wrote them later, from notebooks, when the children were asleep.

Chicken Feathers was written with an old photograph of my mother, taken long before I was born, propped on my desk in front of me. (A photograph, being a framed, static image, is an easy way of starting to write a poem.) Writing about these things made them feel very precious. Life was being observed, as the American poet William Carlos Williams puts it, 'in the belief that it holds a secret'.

In *Dewpond and Black Drainpipes* a dewpond is a shallow pond fed by dew that the Romans used. Drainpipes are tight jeans, made as tight as possible by being worn in a hot bath for a long time.

The Flowers is a poem for my daughter, who was nine when my father died.

Down by the Salley Gardens is another photograph poem, this time comparing my friend as a young bride to the older, sadder person she has become.

Among the Thyme and Daisies was written as a response to a friend of mine who was nearly forty and dreading it. I remembered the novelist and poet Alison Fell's great phrase: 'We will henna our hair like Colette and go out in a last wild blaze'; and I thought, I can't be like that, but, too bad. I'll be lazy and happy instead.

The Goose is about a girl who became a Muslim and brought up her children in Muslim ways; and about her parents and how sad and puzzled they became.

Below Hekla is about one of my first jobs after leaving school, when I went to work in an orphanage in Iceland. The children were very excited about my being English, because that's where the Beatles came from. (Writing is like travelling abroad – everything seems different and special when you start writing about it – so writing about travelling abroad is another easy way into beginning to write.)

The Bicycle Ride, along with *The Flowers*, *Chicken Feathers*, and, indirectly, *The Goose*, is about my father's death. I never told my family or my teachers that I wrote poems, although my father, a writer himself, would have been interested, I'm sure. I think I liked the secretiveness of it, although after the secretiveness comes the sharing, and that is really why we write it seems to me. I hope that reading my poems will encourage some of you to write some poems of your own, to tell us how it is for you.

Chicken Feathers

I

What a picture!
She has tucked her wild-looking chicken
under her arm and stares out
over what seems to be a mountain pass
on a windy day.
She is wearing a blue linen dress
the colour of summer.
She reminds me of Brunhilde –
alone, bronzed, unfamiliar.

10   She doesn't look like anybody's mother.

II

She used to love dancing.
She went to the Chelsea Ball
dressed as a leopard;
there she met my father,
who looked so dashing
in the Harlequin suit
his tailor made for him
from raw silk.
He had tiny shoes

20   like Cinderella's.
I have seen them.

III

She comes to collect me from school,
on time, silent,
and I hand her my coat and satchel –
avoiding, even then, her lovely eyes,
that look down on my world
like distant stars.
I play with the girl next door,
and don't come home till bed-time.

IV

30 From the lighted window
I watch my mother
picking leeks in the twilight.

I will have soup
for my supper,
sprinkled with parsley.

She passes me my creamy bowl.
My hands are warm,
and smell of soap.

My mother's hands are cold as roots.
40 She shuts up the chickens
by moonlight.

V

How can they think I am asleep
when he bends down and kisses
the nape of her neck,
and goes away to his own room,
while she sits in front of her mirror
and brushes and brushes
her waist-long silver hair?

VI

The hens are all gone.
50 How happy she used to be
setting out in her long tweed coat
across the orchard
with her bucket.
Chuck, chuck, chuck, she called
and they'd all come running.

VII

She walks behind the hedges
of the large garden, stooping
from time to time
to pick narcissi
60   for her mother's grave,
now that it is Easter.
We don't want to go.
We're too young to remember
our grandmother –
and besides it will be cold
in the grave-yard
where the wind blows
straight in off the downs.

VIII

He went to his room with an orange
70   in his hand, and died there
sometime during the afternoon.
My mother spent the day in the kitchen.
When I came in from the garden
I was sent upstairs
to call him down to tea:
He was sitting by the window
with his back to me.
On the table beside him
were four boats made of orange peel,
80   with the pith piled neatly inside them.
My mother couldn't stand up.
She kept on saying she was sorry,
but she couldn't stand up.
It must be the shock she said.
It wasn't grief.
Come and sit down she said,
And have your tea.

IX

Tonight I kissed my mother,
for the first time that I can remember;
90   though I must have kissed her before,
as all daughters kiss their mothers.
She was passing in front of me
to kiss the children, and I leant down
and touched her cheek with my lips.
It was easy – like the lighting of a candle.

X

My sister always says
that on the morning our father died
he was working on a drawing of a liner
disappearing over a white horizon.
100   She says it is a symbol.
She's got the picture by her bed.
I would rather think of dying
as a coming into harbour,
a sort of final mooring.

XI

You put in at a little jetty.
There is someone there to welcome you –
not sinister – but rather surprising –
someone you know. In front of you rise
banks of fern and shining celandines.
110   You can smell the woods.
They are full of life,
but very still.

XII

My mother and I, in our way,
understand each other.
When I kneel by her grave,
in need of a little consolation,
I will picture her standing
on a hillside in bright sunlight,
lifting her hand to wave to me;
120 or is she brushing away the feathers
that drift like dreams into her hair
and tickle her cheek, till she smiles.

The Ram

He jangles his keys in the rain
and I follow like a lamb.
His house is as smoky as a dive.
We go straight downstairs to his room.

I lie on his bed and watch him
undress. His orange baseball jacket,
all the way from Ontario,
drops to the floor – THE RAMS, in felt,

arched across the hunky back.
10 He unzips his calf-length
Star-walkers, his damp black Levi's,
and adjusts his loaded modelling-pouch:

he stands before me in his socks –
as white as bridesmaids,
little daisies, driven snow.
John Wayne watches from the wall

beside a shelf-ful of pistols.
Well, he says, *d'you like it?*
All I can think of is Granny,
20 how she used to shake her head,

when I stood by her bed on Sundays,
so proud in my soap-smelling
special frock, and say *Ah,*
Bless your little cotton socks!

Dewpond and Black Drainpipes

In order to distract me, my mother
sent me on an Archaeology Week.
We lived in tents on the downs,
and walked over to the site
every morning. It was an old dewpond.

There was a boy there called Charlie.
He was the first boy I had really met.
I was too shy to go to the pub,
but I hung around the camp every night
10 waiting for him to come back.

He took no notice of me at first,
but one night the two of us
were on Washing-Up together.
I was dressed in a black jersey
and black drain-pipes, I remember.

You in mourning? he said.
He didn't know I was
one of the first beatniks.
He put a drying-up cloth
20 over my head and kissed me

through the linen Breeds of Dogs.

I love you, Charlie I said.
Later, my mother blamed herself
for what had happened. *The Romans
didn't even interest her*, she said.

The Flowers

After lunch my daughter picked
handfuls of the wild flowers
she knew her grandfather liked best
and piled them in the basket of her bicycle,
beside an empty jam-jar and a trowel;
then, swaying like a candle-bearer,
she rode off to the church
and, like a little dog, I followed her.

She cleared the grave of nettles
10   and wild parsley, and dug a shallow hole
to put the jam-jar in. She arranged
the flowers to look their best
and scraped the moss from the stone,
so you could see whose grave
she had been caring for.
It didn't take her long – no longer
than making his bed in the morning
when he had got too old to help her.

Not knowing how to leave him,
20   how to say good-bye, I hesitated
by the rounded grave. *Come on,*
my daughter said, *It's finished now.*
And so we got our bicyles and rode home
down the lane, moving apart
and coming together again,
in and out of the ruts.

Down by the Salley Gardens

You are stamping squares of turf down
with your boots, where you have planted bulbs.
At the open window someone is playing
'Down By the Salley Gardens'
on an old piano, and singing.
You straighten up from time to time
and rub the small of your back.

One of your children puts a wedding album
open on the table, and runs away laughing.
10 Here you are on tiptoe, winding
flowers in your hair. Your new husband
leads you towards a lawnful of ladies
under a shower of confetti. Darling,
you are their bride! How they love you!

A hundred ghosts are watching you
as you come up to the back door
with your bag of bulbs.
You push some hair under your scarf
with hands as muddy as paws.
20 Don't listen to the sad music –
'the weirs... the little snow-white feet... '

Among the Thyme and Daisies

We climbed in bare feet to the barrow –
losing the path, tumbling
over rabbit-holes, turning round
from time to time to see
how small the villages were getting.

We reached the first chalk foot
exhausted. The sky seemed nearer,
friendlier, baby-blue. We walked along
the giant's flowery legs, tickling
10   his fat thighs like ants.

When we found the head,
we closed our eyes and wished –
for something new and wonderful;
we never thought of the Future,
or wished for that.

And now, approaching forty,
I feel like a giantess myself –
vain, drowsy, out-of-date,
ruminating on my hill
20   among the thyme and daisies.

I hear the children holler
down the rabbit-burrows,
and feel them climbing my legs;
there is grass growing over my face,
and a wonderful view of the sky.

The Goose

Rhamia, their only child, is coming home!
Not since the day they kissed her
and she drove away to be a muslim
has there been such life at the Vicarage.
They hurry down to the orchard to call Boo,
the goose. She runs up like a lamb
and pokes her white neck into their basket –
on the look-out for food as usual.
In the kitchen Cook is podding bowls of peas
10 in front of an open recipe book.
Garnish with watercress. Stuff with sage.
She chops up the onions and feels tears
run down her cheeks like mercury.

Rhamia, who used to be called Jenny,
walks out of the drawing-room.
She calls to Abdullah, her son,
Come out to the yard now, and the boy
comes running. His old grand-parents
watch him from the window.
20 He slits the white neck of the goose
with a carving-knife and as the blood
runs over his wrists he calls out
Allah! Allah! His high child's voice
rings out across the fields.
Then he takes the body in to Cook,
who is rolling out pastry in the kitchen.

The Bicycle Ride

I step into the Autumn morning
like a First Communicant
and ride off down the lane,
singing.
Across the frosty fields
someone is mending fences
knock knock knock,
and a twig that's caught
in my bicycle spokes
10   tinkles like a musical box.
The village smells of wood-ash
and warm horses.
Shining crows rise
into the sky like hymns.

I have to pass the church
where my father was buried.
It's a wonderful church.
The Christ in the chancel
is carved by Eric Gill.
20   There are guidebooks in the nave,
and every day the villagers come
to put fresh flowers
on the graves. My father's
is under the yew tree
by the wall. I look at it
out of the corner of my eye
as I go cycling past,
making for open country.

We didn't go this way
30   after the funeral –
my mother and me,

and my sad unfamiliar aunts
crying and crying
for their lost brother.
In hired cars,
we went straight home,
where some kind person
had made us tea
and tiny sandwiches.
40   They were like pocket-handkerchiefs.
Pat, pat, pat... My father
used to dry my tears like that.

Diving at Midnight

She's been diving at midnight
with Harry again,
and this morning she has realized
with a kind of helpless joy
that changes everything,
that she was born to be a diver:
every day until she dies,
she wants to stand,
with nothing but her Speedo on,
10   and stretch into the dive
like a high note; fly beautifully;
and enter the deep water like a die
on which your life depends.

She turns her chair into the sun,
and takes her T-shirt off,
to feel the sun shine on her breasts.
It touches her like sleepy babies
when your milk comes in.
It isn't true, she thinks to herself –

20 letting her mind wander
to the Arctic night,
and a lonely hooded waterfowler singing
to the sky –
it isn't true
that suffering in empty solitudes
is all man has to bring him close to God,

as poor old Igjugarjuk seems to think,
creeping along Prince Albert Sound,
steadying himself
30 on a bone harpoon.
He carried a beaded quiver and a bow.
He's stalking seventeen large geese.
He's listening
for the creaks and groans
of ice collapsing.
Carved goggles made of driftwood
curved by steam
protect his cold eyes
from the polar light

40 that whitens roots
and bones and stiffened hair
and kisses blown
against the wind-blown snow.
His people drift
among the shadows of the glaciers
and comb the hollowed plains
for wolverine and owls.
They're slow. They have to be.
They live curled up,
50 like the blue-glass beads
on the quiver that chink
against the bow-shaft bone.

Below Hekla

I appear like a bird from nowhere.
I have a new name.
I am as clean as a whistle.
I beat the buttermilk in big white bowls
until it is smooth.
I wash the pearly plates under the tap,
and fifty canvas bumpers and fifty socks.
They drip in the sun
below grey mountains like the moon's.

10   Each night I lift the children
in their sleep and hold out
the china pot for them:
Wilt Þú þissa, elskan,
þissa, þissa I whisper
as I tiptoe from bed to bed…
Around mid-night,
I go to the geyser below Hekla
and bathe in the warm water.

I am a short fat English girl.
20   I am twenty-five mothers.
I lead my children in a line
across the heather to the church.
The father watches me
from his dark door.
He shakes his head,
and takes me by the hand:
Blessa Þú, elskan, blessa Þú!

And now, September,
dust is flying: the bus is here.
30 I am ready.
I am on my way to Reykjavik,

Leith, Liverpool…
The children of the Barnaheimilið
are running to the gate like hens.
Good-bye, blessa Þú,
give our love to the Beatles, good-bye.

The Fowlers of the Marshes

Three thousand years ago
they were fowling in the marshes
around Thebes – men in knotted skirts
and tiered faience collars,
who avoided the brown crocodile,
and loved the ibis, which they stalked
with long striped cats on strings,
under the eye of Nut, the goddess of the sky.

My mother's hushed peculiar world's the same:
10 she haunts it like the fowlers of the marshes,
tiptoeing gaily into history, sustained by gods
as strange to me as Lady Nut, and Anubis,
the oracular, the jackal-masked.
When I meet her at the station, I say
Hello, Mum! and think *Hello, Thoth,*
This is the Weighing of the Heart.

Liz Lochhead

The Poet's Introduction

I don't know why I began writing poems, but I can remember working on the first one, how after a visit to a geriatric hospital with a church group I was (but didn't *feel*) part of, I came home with the rhythm and the words of the first four lines singing in my head on the bus journey, not at all as if I'd 'made them up' but as if there-they-were. I wrote them down, then didn't know what else to do... Then next day I got 'flu, and as I recovered, bored with my library books, picked up that pad with those four free-gift lines again. On a sketch pad, no doubt. I was a first-year student at the time, nineteen years old and I had quite deliberately during the hymn singing, been trying to remember the images and the composition of that place full of slack jaws, ties and tremors or blankness and frozen stillness, regimented rows of iron-sided cots squashed too close together. I had been wondering how you could get the smell into drawings or a painting... Four free-gift lines and my boredom disappeared into the excitement of working hard on the chase for the rest of the poem. It wasn't a decision, there didn't seem to be anything else to do but try and find the *rest* of the poem, surprise myself by seeing what I wanted to say, paint this picture with words. (I never made the painting.)

I didn't know it then, but this is the way my many other poems, many other pursuits, have always come about for me. A little bit of free-gift nudging at me (four lines was a lot, and luckier than usual) and then the irresistible, neither hard nor easy, either short or long, but rather more conscious, and certainly more dogged *work* of finishing making the poem. Work that is a real pleasure.

It was a surprise, that first one, because for most of school I had quite a strong distaste for poetry. ''Tis', ''Twas', 'Oh!', 'O!', 'Ah', 'Wert', ludicrous inversions of normal word order, 'thou', 'thee', odes to skylarks, nightingales or Grecian urns, a prickling embarrassment and irritation against those airy-fairy beings who *refused just to put things down in plain English...* No wonder I preferred plays, stories, novels! At the time I didn't realize that the poet is *always*

117

trying to put things down in plain, the *plainest* English, in as short and as clear and as *true* a way as possible. It is just that poems often get made out of yes-and-no, out of our mixed feelings, poems can often mean more-than-one-thing-at-the-same-time.

In my experience, when people ask, 'Do your poems have a message?' they tend to mean, 'Do you have a particular little homily, piece of philosophy to illustrate, political statement to make, moral to illuminate, or general point to make via the anecdotal material of this poem?' And I absolutely *do not think this is what poetry is for*. So when I answer, 'Yes, all my poems have messages – for me,' I mean that until I have written the poem, perhaps not even then, will I know what these 'messages' are. So that, for instance, *The Teachers* and *The Prize* might arguably contain a distaste for the strictures, rigidities and competitiveness of the Scottish Education system, but that isn't why I wrote them. They are, very simply, memories and small ironies (a leather two-split strap 'tawse' for punishment coiled like a snake around the sweetie tin full of equally frequently doled-out rewards for instance). And I have to hope that by being absolutely particular and truthful *for myself*, even to the point of using a word like 'helio' *because Miss Mathieson did*, for the mauve colour that was less popular than blue or pink and the left over one that slowcoaches like me who made heavy going of the hard and tedious needlework were left with – so that even if you, the reader, don't immediately understand mauve for 'helio', you will, I have to hope, recognize the accuracy of the period detail, in an Edwardian-sounding word like 'helio'. ('Helio' is short for heliotrope, a mauve-coloured flower.)

Many other pieces here are similarly personal childhood memories – *The Offering, Poppies, Revelation* – but the reader should beware of assuming that the speaker of a poem, the 'I' voice, is necessarily, the poet. Poems that work and come alive often have a 'persona' that may be very far from the actual character or 'personality' of the poet herself or himself... *Spinster*, for instance, is one of these, (it's usually published with *Bawd* its mirror-opposite and its continuation in a sense). In these poems and in *Storyteller, The Father, The Mother*, and in *Everybody's Mother* – although in none of these is an 'I' voice speaking, but third person singular – I am dealing quite consciously in *archetypes* larger than life, cardboard cut-out kinds of figures that still contain universal truths. We have inside us at the same time many seemingly contradictory roles, or archetypes, and in my second book of poems which was called *The Grimm Sisters*, I enjoyed exploring these.

A Giveaway, is an ironic and ambivalent love poem. A taking-it-all-back, in fact, of another, slightly earlier and more whole-hearted love poem. And it also uses, as a metaphor for the 'making-up feelings' that go on in love affairs, the construction of 'feelings' in writing itself.

Laundrette and *An Abortion* are both reportage of real events in scenes. What I like about *Laundrette* is its rhymes; and with *An Abortion* – what I like about this one is that despite its clumsiness (I threw it away and then rescued it back out of the waste paper basket), it somehow traps some of the power (and ambiguous feelings) of the real event with the real cow outside my window. It tries to say something about responsibility, maybe the specifically female responsibility for creativity itself.

Fat Girl's Confession isn't a poem at all. Just a bit of (maybe painful) fun, an *out loud* rhyme in the music hall humorous recitations style that relishes the stereotype, the cliché, the outrageously convoluted rhyme scheme and overextended rhythm. But then – even back when I thought I disliked 'poetry' – I always loved the 'blood and guts' ballads, the vernacular narratives, the rude and unrespectable rhymes, the 'oral tradition'...

The Offering

Never in a month of them
would you go back.
Sunday,
the late smell of bacon
then the hard small feeling
of the offering in the mitten.
Remember how the hat-elastic cut.
Oh the boredom,
and how a lick of spittle got purple dye or pink
10   from the hymn-book you worried.
Maybe your neighbour would
have technicoloured pictures of
Jesus curing lepers
between the frail tissue pages of her bible
or she'd stroke you with the velvet
of a pressed rosepetal
till someone sucking peppermint
and smelling of mothball
poked you and hissed that you weren't to fidget.
20   Remember the singing
(with words and actions)
and how you never quite
understood the one about Nic-
odemus Coming to the Lord by Night.

Sunday,
perhaps an auntie
would visit with a cousin. Every Sunday
everyone would eat ice cream
and your mothers would compare you,
30   they'd stand you by the doorstop
and measure you up.

Sunday, maybe later in the evening
There'd be a Brethren Meeting.
Plain women wearing hats to cover
uncut hair. And
singing, under lamp-posts, out in our street.
And the leader
shouted the odds on Armageddon, he
tried to sell Salvation.
40 Everybody turned their televisions up.

Never in a month of them
should you go back.
Fond hope.
you'll still find you do not measure up.
The evangelist still mouths behind glass unheard.
You'll still not understand
the singing, the action or the word.
Ice cream will cloy, too sweet, too bland.
And the offering
50 still hard and knotted in your hand.

The Teachers

they taught
that what you wrote in ink
carried more weight than what you wrote in pencil
and could not be rubbed out.
Punctuation was difficult. Wars
were bad but sometimes necessary
in the face of absolute evil as they knew only too well.
Miss Prentice wore her poppy the whole month
    of November.

Miss Mathieson hit the loud pedal
10   on the piano and made us sing
The Flowers of the Forest.
Miss Ferguson deplored the Chinese custom
of footbinding but extolled the ingenuity
of terracing the paddyfields.
Someone she'd once known had given her a kimono
    and a parasol.
Miss Prentice said the Empire had enlightened people
and been a two way thing.
The Dutch grew bulbs and were our allies in
wooden shoes.

20   We grew bulbs on the window sills
beside the frogspawn that quickened into wriggling
commas or stayed full stop.
Some people in our class were stupid, full stop.
The leather tawse was coiled around the sweetie tin
in her desk beside the box of coloured blackboard chalk
Miss Ferguson never used.
Miss Prentice wore utility smocks.
Miss Mathieson had a moustache.
If your four-needled knitting got no
30   further than the heel you couldn't turn
then she'd keep you at your helio sewing
till its wobbling cross-stitch was specked with rusty
    blood.

Spelling hard words was easy when you knew how.

The Prize

for Perfect Attendance was an easy one to win.
Bible stories for girls. Martha and Mary on the coloured
    frontispiece.
Your Sunday name in the Superintendent's copperplate.

It meant being there, not 'paying attention',
The Redemption hymnbook proved
the devil did not possess every best tune.

Red ticks like flyaway
flocks of birds sprigged the best exercise books.
Gold stars were favours given seldom as boiled sweets
10 in crinkled cellophane. X's were kisses
and kissing was wrong as all my sums.
Being first was top desk.
The doltish and dirty shared front row
with one sent down clever chatterbox in easy reach
of the teacher's ruler.

That September the squirrel
on the Shell country calendar wasn't on the wall
before Mattie won first death.
The weather chart said Today it is Cloudy
20 and my Top in General Knowledge
came of knowing the name for such a cloud
was Cumulus. We had to all turn over our jotters
and go over and over once again
till we knew by heart the Highway Code.

Revelation

I remember once being shown the black bull
when a child at the farm for eggs and milk.
They called him Bob – as though perhaps
you could reduce a monster
with the charm of a friendly name.
At the threshold of his outhouse, someone
held my hand and let me peer inside.
At first, only black
and the hot reek of him. Then he was immense,
10   his edges merging with the darkness, just
a big bulk and a roar to be really scared of,
a trampling, and a clanking tense with the chain's jerk.
His eyes swivelled in the great wedge of his tossed head.
He roared his rage. His nostrils gaped.

And in the yard outside,
oblivious hens picked their way about.
The faint and rather festive tinkling
behind the mellow stone and hasp was all they knew
of that Black Mass, straining at his chains.
20   I had always half-known he existed –
this antidote and Anti-Christ his anarchy
threatening the eggs, well rounded, self-contained –
and the placidity of milk.

I ran, my pigtails thumping on my back in fear,
past the big boys in the farm lane
who pulled the wings from butterflies and
blew up frogs with straws.
Past thorned hedge and harried nest,
scared of the eggs shattering –
30   only my small and shaking hand on the jug's rim
in case the milk should spill.

Laundrette

We sit nebulous in steam.
It calms the air and makes the windows stream
rippling the hinterland's big houses to a blur
of bedsits – not a patch on what they were before.

We stuff the tub, jam money in the slot,
sit back on rickle chairs not
reading. The paperbacks in our pockets curl.
Our eyes are riveted. Our own colours whirl.

We pour in smithereens of soap, The machine sobs
10   through its cycle. The rhythm throbs
and changes. Suds drool and slobber in the churn.
Our duds don't know which way to turn.

The dark shoves one man in,
lugging a bundle like a wandering Jew. Linen
washed in public here.
We let out of the bag who we are.

This youngwife has a fine stack of sheets, each pair
a present. She admires their clean cut air
of colourschemes and being chosen. Are the dyes fast?
20   This christening lather will be the first test.

This woman is deadpan before the rinse and sluice
of the family in a bagwash. Let them stew in their juice
to a final fankle, twisted, wrung out into rope,
hard to unravel. She sees a kaleidoscope

For her to narrow her eyes and blow smoke at, his overalls
and pants ballooning, tangling with her smalls
and the teeshirts skinned from her wriggling son.
She has a weather eye for what might shrink or run.

This dour man does for himself. Before him,
30   half lost, his small possessions swim.
Cast off, random
they nose and nudge the porthole glass like flotsam.

An Abortion

The first inkling I had of the beast's agony
was the something not right
of her scrabbling, scrabbling
to still not quite find
all four feet.
Sunk again, her cow-tongue lolled
then spiked the sky, she rolled
great gape-mouth, neck distended
in a Guernica of distress.
10   That got through to me all right
behind glass as I was
a whole flat field away.
It took an emblem-bellow
to drag me from my labour
at the barbed words on my desk top.

Close to, green foam flecked her muzzle
and drizzled between the big bared brown teeth.
Spasms, strong, primeval
as the pulsing locomotion of some
20   terrible underwater creature,
rippled down her flank
and her groan was the more awesome
for being drier, no louder than a cough.

When she tried to rise again
I saw it.
Membrane wrapped, the head of a calf
hung out, and the wrong-looking bundle
of a knuckle. Then her rope-tail dropped
and she fell back on it, steamrollering it
30   under her.

When the summoned men came,
buttoning blue coveralls over
the Sunday lunches and good-suit waistcoats,
they wound string around one man's knuckles
meant business and the
curt thank-you-very-much of the other
dismissed me.

Shamed voyeur, back at my notebooks again
my peeled eyes caught the quick hoick
40   of the string loop, the dead thing flopping
to the grass, the cow on her knees and
up again, the men leaving, one
laughing at some punchline.

The thing is this. Left alone,
that cow licking at those lollop limbs
which had not formed properly
with her long tongue,
that strong tongue,
which is a match for thistles
50   and salt-lick coarse as pumice stone
tenderly over and over again at
what has come out of her and she is responsible for
as if she can not believe it will not
come alive,
not if she licks long enough.

Outside she is still licking, licking
till in the blue dusk
the men in blue come back again
and she turns, goes quietly with them
60   as if they were policemen
and she knew exactly what she was guilty of.

Poppies

My father said she'd be fined
at best, jailed maybe, the lady
whose high heels shattered the silence.
I sat on his knee, we were listening
to the silence on the radio.
My mother tutted, oh that it was terrible,
as over our air
those sharp heeltaps struck steel, rang clear
as a burst of gunfire or a laugh
10   through those wired-up silent streets around the Cenotaph.
Respect.
Remembrance.
Surely when all was said
two minutes silence in November
wasn't much to ask for, for the dead?
Poppies on the mantelpiece, the photograph
of a boy in a forage cap, the polished
walnut veneer of the wireless,
the buzzing in the ears and when
20   the silence ended the heldfire voice
of the commentator, who was shocked,
naturally, but not
wanting to make too much of it.
Why did she do it?

Was she taken sick – but that was no
excuse, on the radio it said,
couldn't you picture it?
how grown soldiers buttoned in their uniforms
keeled over, fell like flies
30 trying to keep up the silence.
Maybe it was looking at the khaki button eye
and the woundwire stem
of the redrag poppy
pinned in her proper lapel
that made the lady stick a bloody bunch of them
behind her ear
and clash those high heels across the square,
a dancer.

A Giveaway

I cancelled out the lines that most let on
I loved you. One week after I thought that it was done
and perfect, practically in print – here goes again
more of this that amateurs think of as tampering.
The tripe that's talked at times, honestly –
about truth and not altering a word,
being faithful to what you felt, whatever
that is, the 'First Thought's Felicity'.
I have to laugh… the truth!
10 You and me and no reason
for me to imagine I know the half of it.
I've said it time and time again,
listen, you've got to be ruthless,
if the rhythm's not right, it's not right,
it's simple
you've got to cut and cut and cut.
Rewrite.

Today's fair copy skips the scored out bit.
And all the better for it. That verse
20 set in the bedroom spoilt the form
and was never the issue anyway. Irrelevant.
At any rate I've gone to town on it all right
with black biro, blocked it out – hay
fever sneeze spill and kiss are all
the words even I can make out of it now.
Never could cancel with a single stroke!
Oh maybe it is a giveaway but don't
please be naïve enough to think I'd mind
your knowing what I might invent of what I feel.
30 Poets don't bare their souls, they bare their skill.
God, all this
long apprenticeship and still
I can't handle it, can't
make anything much of it, that's my shame.
It's not an easy theme.
But finally I've scrubbed it, faced it, I know
the whole bloody stanza was wonky from the word go.

The Other Woman

The other woman
lies
between us like a bolster.
When I hit out wild she's
insubstantial a
flurry of feathers a mere
sneezing irritant.
When my shaped and hardened words turn
machine-gun
10 against you she's rock solid
the sandbag you hide behind.

The other woman
lies
when she says she does not want
your guts for her garterbelt.
I send out spies, they say relax
she's a hag she's just a kid
she's not a patch she's nothing to she's
no oil painting.
20   I'd know her anywhere.
I look for her in department stores, I scan
every cinema-queue.
Sometimes suddenly in some downtown restaurant
I catch her eye
casting crazily around for me.

The other woman
lies
the other side of my very own mirror.
Sweet, when I smile
30   straight out for you, she
puts a little twist on it, my
right hand never knows what her left is doing.
She's sinister.
She does not mean you well.

Storyteller

she sat down
at the scoured table
in the swept kitchen
beside the dresser with its cracked delft.
And every last crumb of daylight was salted away.

No one could say the stories were useless
for as the tongue clacked
five or forty fingers stitched
corn was grated from the husk
10   patchwork was pieced
or the darning done.

Never the one to slander her shiftless.
Daily sloven or spotless no matter whether
dishwater or tasty was her soup.
To tell the stories was her work.
It was like spinning,
gathering thin air to the singlest strongest
thread. Night in
she'd have us waiting, held
20   breath, for the ending we knew by heart.

And at first light
as the women stirred themselves to build the fire
as the peasant's feet felt for clogs
as thin grey washed over flat fields
the stories dissolved in the whorl of the ear
but they
hung themselves upside down
in the sleeping heads of the children
till they flew again
30   in the storytellers night.

The Father

loving and bungling,
offending the evil fairy by forgetting
her invitation to the Christening,
or being tricked into bartering his beloved daughter
in exchange for the rose he only
took to please her –
then compounding it all
by over-protectiveness and suppression
(banning
10 spinning wheels indeed
when the sensible thing would have been
to familiarize her from the cradle
and explain their power to hurt her).

But when she comes,
the beautiful daughter,
leading her lover by the sleeve, laughing –
'Come and meet my daddy, the King,
he's absolutely a hundred years behind the times
but such a dear.'
20 and she's (note Redeeming Kiss)
wide-eyed and aware.
Stirring, forgiven, full of love and terror,
her father hears her footstep on the stair.

The Mother

is always two faced.
At best, she wished you
into being. Yes, it was she
cried at the seven drops of blood that fell,
staining the snow – she
who bargained crazily with Fate
for that longawaited child
as red as blood
as white as snow
10   and when you came true it was
she who clapped her hands merrily because
she was as happy as a Queen could be.
But she's always dying early,
so often it begins to look deliberate.
abandoning you,
leaving you to the terrible mercy
of the Worst Mother. The one who married your father.
She doesn't like you, she
prefers all your sisters, she
20   loves her sons.
She's jealous of mirrors.
She wants your heart in a casket.
When she cuts the apple in two and selflessly
takes the sour green half
she's good and glad to see you poisoned
by the sweet red pulp.
Tell me
what kind of prudent parent
would send a little child on a foolish errand in the forest
30   with a basket jammed with goodies
and wolf-bait? Don't trust her an inch.

Spinster

This is no way to go on.
Get wise. Accept. Be
a spinister of this parish.
My life's in shards.
I will keep fit in leotards.

Go vegetarian. Accept.
Support good causes.
Be frugal, circumspect.
Keep cats. Take tidy fits.
10 Go to evening classes.
Keep a nest-egg in the bank.
Try Yoga. Cut your losses.
Accept. Admit you're a bit of a crank –

Oh I may be a bit of a crank
but still I get by, frugally. Think positive.
I live and let live. Depend
on nobody. Accept.
Go in for self-improvement.
Keep up with trends.
20 I'll cultivate my conversation.
I'll cultivate my friends.
I'll grow a herbaceous border.
By hook by crook I'll get my house in order.

Everybody's Mother

Of course
everybody's mother always and
so on...

Always never
loved you enough
or too smothering much.

Of course you were the Only One, your
mother
a machine
10   that shat out siblings, listen

everybody's mother
was the original Frigid-
aire Icequeen clunking out
the hardstuff in nuggets, mirror-
silvers and ice-splinters that'd stick
in your heart.

Absolutely everyone's mother
was artistic when she was young.

Everyone's mother
20   was a perfumed presence with pearls, remote
white shoulders when she
bent over in her ball dress
to kiss you in your crib.

Everybody's mother slept with the butcher
for sausages to stuff you with.

Everyone's mother
mythologized herself. You got mixed up
between dragon's teeth and blackmarket stockings.

Naturally
30 she failed to give you
Positive Feelings
about your own sorry
sprouting body (it was a bloody shame)

but she did
sit up all night sewing sequins
on your carnival costume

so you would have a good time

and she spat
on the corner of her hanky and scraped
40 at your mouth with sour lace till you squirmed

so you would look smart

And where
was your father all this time?
Away
at the war, or
in his office, or any-
way conspicuous for his
Absence, so

what if your mother did
float around above you
50 big as a barrage balloon
blocking out the light?

Nobody's mother can't not never do nothing right.

Fat Girl's Confession

(Rap)

Roll up and see the Fat Lady!
Such a jolly sight to see.
Seems my figure is a Figure of Fun...
To everyone but me.

Smile! Say Cottage Cheese!
You all know me –
I'm the Office Fat Girl, the one you see
Wearing Vast Dark Dresses and a Cheery Veneer...
And lingerie constructed by a civil engineer.

10   Occasionally, you meet some bloke who'll give you this
       tripe
About how, yeuch, he's repelled by the skinny model type.
He can't see the attraction, he'll swear by all he owns
It'd be like lying in bed with a rickle of bones.
But, oh how he *lurrves*
Yir Voluptuous Curves
And your Supper Board that Groans.

I met him at my wee cousin's wedding – he was the Best
       Man
– he says to me would you like to go out for a bite to eat? I
mean, do you fancy a curry? A Chinese? An Italian? I said,
20   who me? Oh, I love...

Lasagne and canne-linguini and *pasta* and stuff.
(well, who with pasta, ever says basta,
enough!)
And then for my *main* course I tend to choose
something smothered in a sauce made of butter, cream
       and booze
with asparagus hollandaise and cauliflower mornay

potatoes dauphines, onion rings and mushrooms saute.
And after the cheeseboard, my sweet tooth's nagging, so
I need another great big stodgy wedge of Blackforest
    Gateau.
30 Well, when it comes to pudding,
the way I see it –
with cheesecake you've got a choice:
Either EAT it or BE it.

I didnae cry when he left me
I gave not one cheep, not a chirrup –
just devoured a whole packet of Mr Kipling's Kunzle Cakes
and a half hundredweight sack of Mexicali Taco chips
    dunked in Maplesyrup.
went for a double blackpudding supper, then half an
    hour later,
I ravished the refrigerator
40 (in my classic response to Rejection and Pain)
and immediately began eating
My Heart Out again.

But, Oh
Dear Joe,
much as I miss you
I just been reading how Fat Is A Feminist Issue.
Fat Girls like me have all fallen from grace –
If I could feed my own ego I wouldnae need to feed my
    face!
Everyone needs Oral Satisfaction, but
50 the Truly Fulfilled don't need a filled-full gut.
I says, Enough of this Junk food, You Are What You Eat.
When did you last see your lover?
When did you last see your feet?
So… I'm persevering, but it's kind of hard
to live on lettuce, and self-regard.

But, you know, I've been really, really, good today!
Breakfast was black coffee, plus a saccharine tab from the
    tube.
For my lunch, a half-a-cup of chicken bullion made with a
Knorr chicken stock-cube.

60   Dinner: two slice of starch-reduced Ryvita
with a scrape of slimmer's imitation margarine,
then I pedalled myself blue in the face on the Exercise
    Machine.
See, I've joined this Health Club, and hell, I
saw some sights you wouldnae believe!
Enough heaving flesh to make you heave.
All that pummelling, and pedalling, and pounding, and
    sweating
and keeking in the mirror to see how much thinner
    you're getting!
Well, there's not one lady Waging the Inch War or
    wielding the tape
who doesnae wish for a Dishy Man to lick her inty
    shape.

70   So I'm stuck here in this Stephanie Bowman Sweat-It-Off
    Slimmersuit
I feel a right clown!
I'm to huff, I'm to puff.
I'll *wear* my hips down.
I'll mortify my surplus flesh.
remove it like a tumour…
and all to make of myself the kind of confection
who'll appeal to the Consumer?

Notes

Poems by Gillian Clarke

Letter from a Far Country

'In 1978 I wrote a long poem, *Letter From a Far Country*, about a woman who, in the spirit of feminist rebellion, threatens to leave home and family, although in the end seduced by memory, tradition and the ties of family she stays.'

Gillian Clarke, *Poetry Review* Vol 73 No. 2, 1983

The letter is to the men in the poem, *husbands, fathers, forefathers* (8) as an answer to their question, 'Where are your great works?'. The poem suggests an explanation: that women's energies go into daily routine, looking after home and family – and that is, itself, a great work, unfinished until the woman's life comes to an end.

> this is my apologia, my
> letter home from the future,
> my bottle in the sea which might
> take a generation to arrive. (9–12)

> Today this letter goes unsigned,
> unfinished, unposted.
> When it is finished
> I will post it from a far country. (391–394)

The *far country* is 'childhood, womanhood, Wales, the beautiful country where the warriors, kings and presidents don't live, the private place where we all grow up.' (see Gillian Clarke's poet's introduction pp. 1–3). It could also be the territory of the imagination – to which escape is possible, even while caught up in family responsibilities – or the afterlife.

Escape is envisaged, and some of the women in the poem do escape. The *woman who had everything* (289) takes her life; the woman who kept a smallholding does the same, for different reasons. The poem asserts, however, that for those who embrace life

141

and love there is no complete freedom from the great and mysterious forces that govern women's lives:

> We are hawks trained to return
> to the lure from the circle's
> far circumference. Children sing
> that note that only we can hear. (377–380)

It is worth looking at the sequence of events, the structuring of reflections, the evocations of domestic settings, the use of family history and how these are related to and expressed via the imagery the poet uses. What does the poem gain from the 'I', the personal, specific focus of the speaker?

   9 **apologia**   a written defence of the writer's opinions.

  14 **detritus**   untidy clutter (produced in this case by the family).

  44 **Bryn Isaf**   the poet's grandmother's farm was known as 'Lower Hill'.

  46 **under Calfaria's single eye**   the chapel's round window: Cyclops-like.

  89 **chenille**   velvety material.

  92 **Taid**   North Welsh word for grandfather.

  93 **Mellte**   the river Mellte. An onomatopoeic word in Welsh suggesting the rushing of river water.

 120 **Mamgu**   South Welsh word for grandmother.

        pais   Welsh for petticoat.

 190 **blancoed**   whitened.

 191 **daps**   dialect word for plimsolls.

 232 **carder**   someone who disentangles wool for spinning.

 348 **ballast**   heavy material placed in a ship's hold to steady the ship.

 349 **Equinox**   the time when day and night are equal.

354–6 See *St Matthew* 22, 15–22: *Then pay, Caesar what is due to Caesar, and pay God what is due to God* (*St Matthew* 22, 21).

 359 **Nain**   North Welsh word for grandmother.

 358 **Ceredigion**   Cardigan in West Wales.

 371 **Diaconnydd**   deacon (Welsh). A person who assists a Minister.

        Trysorydd   treasurer, in Welsh.

 404 *Mam iaith*   mother tongue.

Miracle on St David's Day

People in the poem are depicted as enclosed and imprisoned: *In a cage of first March sun* (12). This poem is about a dumb labourer's 'escape' from silence; the miraculous finding of a voice during a poetry reading. The whole occasion has something of a 'religious' quality: the gentleness of the staff, the disabilities of the audience who are not full members of the society we inhabit, and the recognition, on everyone's part, that they were witnessing a moment of great significance and mystery.

In Wordsworth's poem the speaker is saved from melancholic isolation by the experience of seeing the daffodils. Not fully realizing at the time what comfort and delight the memory would continue to bring, the poem suggests that the imagination works on experience and creates an escape from self into joy.

The labourer in this poem is the fourth patient mentioned. His importance is signalled by the detail the poet uses: he is *tenderly led* (15), he *has never spoken* (16), *hands on his knees, he rocks/gently to the rhythms of the poems* (17–18). The poet reads to everyone, but singles him out: *I read to their presences, absences,/to the big, dumb labouring man as he rocks* (19–20), and he responds.

The labourer's voice, *Like slow/movement of spring water or the first bird/of the year in the breaking darkness* (22–24), is likened to elemental change, the moment of seasonal change and the piercing of darkness by birdsong. In two and a half lines the labourer has been transformed into a sign and witness that there are powerful and unexplained forces that language and Nature can unlock.

Colour is important in this poem. At the beginning yellow is used to evoke the afternoon, not the flowers alone, though later their creams and yellows are noted. They become *flame* at the end. Why?

In *Miracle*, the flowers become listeners, *still as wax... their syllables/unspoken* (28–30). When the labourer finishes, the audience pauses: *we observe/the flowers' silence* (36–37). What does this silence mean? Why does the thrush sing? How does Gillian Clarke prepare the reader for this ending?

> 12 **first March sun** St David's Day is celebrated in Wales on the first of March.
> 32 **by rote** learnt by repetition.

Login

Like *Miracle on St David's Day*, this poem has as its focus a moment of revelation.

Login is described as having only a chapel and bridge, a river bordered with cow parsley and woods that tumble into the valley. The bridge and the cow parsley, however, are used to heighten and make explicit the moment of shared understanding between the 'I' narrator of the poem and the old lady.

Gillian Clarke's comment that: 'Much is said by leaving the rest unsaid' is particularly apt in this case. There is a sense of the cottage interior, the passage, the lace cloth; but the key moment is the one in which the old lady ruffles the boy's hair and the focus is on her veined hands. The river in the village is echoed in phrases like *fast water in her wrists* (14), and *such giddy water* (16), suggesting emotional turmoil but also the passing of time and the way in which streams separate.

The poem ends with the boy bathed in bright sunlight watched by the two women sharing *the brilliance without words* (20) – the realization that the old lady and the poet's father had loved one another. As in *Miracle on St David's Day*, the moment is heightened by the description of flowers and light: *The bridge burns with cow parsley* (19), and *sunlight concentrates/blindingly on the bridge* (23–24).

There is a suggestion that the past is being intensely relived, has been resurrected by the meeting of the two women – and indeed that any notion of what is past, present or future loses meaning in such moments of intense feeling.

25 **sepia** dark, reddish brown colour.

The Sundial

Time, light and shadow are central to this poem as in *Miracle on St David's Day* and *Login*. The sun is *caged* (23), the lions in Owain's dreams roam free. Both Owain and his mother are creatures bounded by time. The *black stick* (24) is a reminder of death.

23 **diurnal** daily.

Marged

This poem is a meditation about the house's previous occupant. As in *Letter from a Far Country* there is the belief that presences, ghosts of previous generations remain. The two women's lives are very different, but they share the house, the garden and its outlook towards the hills, and being women.

> 3 **parlŵr**   the front room, used mainly on Sunday for visitors in the traditional Welsh way.

Overheard in County Sligo

The opening two lines of the poem were in fact overheard by the poet. The fictional woman in the poem at one time had plans and ambitions of her own, but has sacrificed them in order to marry and lead the sort of life she felt was expected of her.

Sligo was a place familiar to and loved by the Irish poet, William Butler Yeats (1865–1939). Much of his childhood was spent there. The form and metre Gillian Clarke uses in this poem are typical of the rhythms Yeats uses, particularly in his early poetry.

> 9 **the Abbey stage**   the Abbey Theatre in Dublin staged Irish plays, some by W. B. Yeats.
> 14 **lustre**   pottery with metallic glaze, often jugs, sometimes china dogs.

East Moors

This poem looks at change in a community, the sort of change some might regard as 'progress' but which the poem suggests can undermine communities, individual identity and purpose.

> Demolition gangs
> erase skylines whose hieroglyphs
> recorded all our stories.   (18–20)

The seasonal change, the arrival of spring blossom, is a device used to suggest a possible end to bitter times at the poem's beginning, but this is undermined by the final verse, where there is *icy/rain* (26–27), the town is *quieter, cleaner, poorer* (28) and the sky is *blind* (30).

Last Rites

Gillian Clarke refers to the accident in her introduction (see p. 2). The driver of the lorry had lost his way and had stopped, not realizing that the motor cyclist and his passenger, riding pillion, had also stopped directly behind him. The lorry driver put the lorry into reverse and moved backwards, leaving the young man on the bike time enough only to throw his passenger clear.

The choice of religious terms is important in this poem. The poet is cast, by circumstance and inclination as the 'priest' who administers the last rites: *I cover him with the grey blanket/From my bed* (15–16). The road continues to bear the marks, 'stigmata' of death, 'dust' – and life in the barley seeds. In fact, the whole poem derives much of its force from the recognition that life continues even after great tragedy, that death and new life seem to come together.

The details of the accident's immediate aftermath are clipped and brief – the man's pulse is *dangerous* (6), *a mains hum* (7). There are other surprising and powerful images, for example, in the description of the motorbike as *Dead as a black horse in a war* (10) and *his fear... like the scream/Of a jet in an empty sky* (13–14).

The contrast of these powerful images with that of the child putting her toys to bed and tucking them in is disturbing and suddenly cut short by the mention of blood on the poet's hands and her comforting of the man's girl-friend. The choice of *cariad* (18) is a good one in that it explains her worth to him and hints at the immensity of her loss.

The poem's final five lines show a landscape that for all its sun and brightness reflects their feelings. The scene is one of death, *shattering* (21) seas, while the sun seems to hurl stones.

> 3 **stigmata** marks corresponding to Christ's wounds appearing without apparent cause on someone's body.
> 18 **cariad** darling (Welsh).

Still Life

Polishing brass presents an opportunity for working together and re-establishing a relationship on a better footing. The extended metaphor, the removing of tarnish from brass objects in the house and the revealing of their patterns under the dirt, is not seen as a complete answer. The objects remain *separate* (29) and *cold* (28), reflecting, like people, warmth shown to each other. What does this poem suggest about people's need for one another?

White Roses

This poem shows Gillian Clarke, again, writing about death. Colour, here white and red, the passing of time and the way in which the natural world seems oblivious to human suffering, all figure in the poem. The image of the roses *like cups of fine, white china* (4) have as their counterpart, within the house, the sick child within whom death is beginning to bloom.

Poems by Grace Nichols

Sugar Cane

18 **ague**   malarial fever.

I Coming Back

12 **higue**   A Guyanese folklore character: an old lady who flies around at night searching for victims whose blood she sucks.

In My Name

In this powerful and tender poem a slave woman is bringing her child into the world uttering charms to protect it. She commands the earth to receive her child in her name, not in the name of any god, and even though it is 'tainted', half negro, half white – she asserts the child's perfection because it has been 'cleansed' by her blood and has a lake to swim in created from her tears and the waters of the Niger.

What metaphors are used to describe the child?

6 **plantain**   tropical tree with fruit like the banana.
18 **mulatto**   child of a white and negro.

147

Caribbean Woman Prayer

Again, the speaker is a woman who commands. This time it is God who is told to listen. She has a vision soundly based on religious principles and her own observations. She is persuasive, positive, and hopeful, in spite of the hardship she, her family and others are experiencing.

Repetition is an important device in this poem, the language the woman uses imitating and modifying passages from the liturgy (the words used in Church services), 'God the Father, God the Son, and God the Holy Ghost.' The repeated use of *You know* and *I want* help keep her argument clear and establish her as a character who has experienced, reflected and arrived at a picture of how her society should be.

Look too at the similes and metaphors the woman uses – *is not we nature/to behave like yard fowl* (33–34) and *suffer us not/to walk in de rags of doubt* (45–46).

16 **pickney** child.
69 **hibiscus** rose mallow plant.

Be a Butterfly

This episode from the poet's childhood is related with considerable economy. The message is laughed at, then reasserted, and the characters are created in a handful of words. The use of language is fresh and skilful: the congregation *sat shaking with muffling/laughter* (10–11) as the preacher expanded *his well-earned/sweat* (6–7).

17 **fufu** dough made with corn meal and sometimes with cassava, pounded into paste. It is cooked in hot water. Also known as 'coo coo'.
pigtail raw, salted, cured pig's tail.

Those Women

3 **seines** large, vertical fishing nets with floats and weights.

Praise Song for My Mother

This is another poem where repetition is used, in words and form. The last part of the poem breaks with the established pattern. Why?

The mothers in *In My Name* and *Praise Song for My Mother* share the recognition that children have their own way to make in the world. Where do you discover this in *Praise Song*?

    6 **mantling**   cloaking.

Iguana Memory

Iguana Memory depicts a small incident which is vividly captured in words. The use of alliteration, repetition – *big* is used three times in one line (6) – and unusual word order all contribute to make the episode 'real'.

Poems by Fleur Adcock

Loving Hitler

This poem creates the scene with great economy of language. The use of dialogue is well calculated, the suspense of waiting for the radio broadcast exploited by the child seeking attention.

It is not necessary to attribute conversation to specific characters in the poem. Why not? There is a paring down to essentials. Most of the poem explores the mind of the child and its sharp insight into the fascist mind: *one thing you could say for Hitler, / you never heard him laugh at people* (24–25).

    2 **Lord Haw-Haw**   During the Second World War William Joyce (Lord Haw-Haw) broadcast propaganda from London for the Germans in an attempt to undermine British morale. He was later executed for treason.

   12 **proto**   first.
      neo   new.

Outwood

> What I remember about Outwood School is terror and poetry.
> The terror was inflicted, as so often, by boys: in a routine tickling
> raid on the girls they discovered I was abnormally afraid of being
> tickled − I was convinced I would lose my breath and die − so
> they tended to lie in wait for me at playtime and lunchtime. The
> three teachers took their lunch in the head's house next door,
> leaving the children to tickle each other to death. To avoid this I
> lurked in the playground shed and wrote poetry.
>
> Fleur Adcock, Poetry Review, Vol. 74, No. 2, 1984

The poem's first stanza uses description of flowers as a way of leading
the reader into the child's experience. It also creates a child who is
observant, who has the time and inclination to notice pollen, grass
heads, different flowers.

The child's solitariness at school, and a desire for company come
through in the second verse. The 'friend' in the poem is male − and
this is echoed later in the poem by Doris and her soldier. Doris, like
the child, has an idea of the appropriate place for romance − and
also, like the child, wishes to experience her young man's company
without the children around. The absorbed behaviour of the couple
lying talking in the grass and their murmurings to each other are
beautifully conveyed in the detail of the pink blouse, the colour of
briar or dog rose blossom, and the likening of their voices to the
softness and roundness of petals.

> 26 **tussore**   strong but coarse silk.

Earlswood

This poem is drawn from experiences when the poet was eleven. It
was still wartime and weapons known as Doodlebugs used to fly over
Earlswood where Fleur Adcock's family were living at the time.

> These ' …pilotless aircraft… chugged up from the south coast towards
> London until their engines cut out, whereupon after a few seconds'
> menacing silence they fell out of the sky… ' Mother seemed to find them
> worrying. She bought a Morrison shelter − a large rectangular iron

structure that sat in the living room, to serve as a dining table by day and a shelter by night. Bedtime became a cosy, communal affair: lying under the shelter on our mattresses we drank cocoa and ate toast and chatted until Mother joined us; then she bolted on the wire mesh anti-shrapnel walls, and we felt perfectly safe (she didn't; she knew better: a direct hit would have done for us all)...

When there was an air-raid warning at school we all marched into the shelters tunnelled under the playground and sat singing 'Ten Green Bottles', which was all that one sang... in shelters, until the All-Clear...

Even we felt sobered, though, when an old lady with a broken arm and lacerations from splinters of glass came to join us on the living room floor; a Doodlebug had fallen a few streets away.

Poetry Review, Vol. 74 No. 2, 1984

A three line stanza has been used in this poem. What do you notice about the line endings? Why do some of the stanzas run on into the next, and to what effect? Why the last, single line?

Tadpoles

A poem about wonder that combines observation of tadpoles' development and reflections on a human child's (the poet's grandson's) development in the womb. The similarities between tadpole and child are brought out, pointing to what we have in common with other life forms. This sense of closeness with the natural world is also encountered in *Last Song*. On the page, tadpoles become *cloudy/compacted spheres* (16–17) *polka dots of blackness* (17), *commas* (18), and then creatures with *animated match heads* (19), *black thread legs* (1), *mini-miniature shoulders, elbows, knees* (2), *rippling smoothness* (4), *fingers/like hair-stubble* (6–7), *clumps-of-eyelashes feet* (7). And in the third stanza there is a rejoicing in the sound of words, *glory from globes of slithery glup* (15).

The child's *dreamy sphere* (22) is the amniotic sac of cloudy water within the womb, in which the foetus lives until just before birth.

There is a lot going on in this poem – the mother's imaginings of her unborn child, the grandmother's separation from daughter and grandson, the passing of time, the poet's reverence for and close observation of the *flickering flock* (20).

   3 **piquant**   sharp.
   24 **avatars**   incarnations of God on Earth.
   34 **effloration**   bursting into flower.

For Heidi with Blue Hair

How is direct speech used in this piece? What is the speaker's attitude to the teachers, and how do you know this?

The Telephone Call

What happens in this poem might equally well be told in story form. How might it differ? Why does the poem form work so effectively?

The Chiffonier

The rhyming couplets and iambic pentameter give this poem a jauntiness even though it anticipates the mother's death. Can you identify any points at which the regular rhythms are broken? What effect do these create?

The poem also shows us the mother of the *Earlswood* poem over forty years later. The frankness and affection between mother and daughter is touching – but does the chosen form of the poem undermine this?

   1 **chiffonier**   moveable low cupboard.
   45 **feijoa**   small tree (feijoa sellowiana) of the Myrtle family, closely related to the guava.

The Keepsake

Regular stanzas, using pentameter again – and a rhyme scheme for a poem which changes mood a little more than halfway through. How does the metre change at the *storm* (33), and the line where the book is inherited (34, 35)? The suddeness of the man's death is driven home by the steady rhythm: *The date in it's five weeks ago tonight* (36).

    10 **demoniac**   devilish, fiendish.
38–39 **nox perpetua**   perpetual night, death.

The Prize-winning poem

    11 **elegies**   poetic lamentations for the dead.
    19 **myriad**   countless.
    21 **archaisms**   phrases, expressions no longer in common use that seem antiquated.
        inversions   reversal of word order.

Last Song

    21 **skew-wiff**   crooked.

Poems by Carol Rumens

At Puberty

In the introduction to her poems on pp. 73–75, Carol Rumens mentions the hopelessness of her love for her music teacher but that there had been, even so, 'intense and wonderful feelings.' The first eleven lines of *At Puberty* suggest the new vision and insights that being in love can bring. The perspective is both the young girl's and the mature woman's looking back on the experience. The insights are suggested by the personification of the asphalt, a new vitality in the Bernadette Grotto and the mulberry tree, and the girl's new ability to contemplate her childhood. Later the girl's love is described as a *miracle* (29), the woman she loves as a *vision* (34) that will *suddenly vanish* (36) leaving her like a *speechless peasant* (35) with an *enormous grief* (37). The language of religion is being used to describe human, not divine love.

    The teacher's indifference to the girl's feelings is suggested in her coquettishness and *merciless* (20) arpeggios. She is, like the Lady of the Manor, aloof and separate.

19 **Bösendorfer**   German make of piano.
20 **coquettishness**   flirtatiousness.
21 **arpeggios**   notes in chords, played in succession.

A Dream of South Africa

The opening stanza with its sea metaphor suggests how completely the sea controlled the man's outlook – the poet's father. The rest of the poem reveals his imaginary world, full of false hopes and plans that grow increasingly difficult to sustain. In the last two stanzas Rumens uses a ship image to suggest what had gone wrong for him and why. The last line has her father sailing towards darkness and death.

29 **Bantu**   an African people.

Over the Bridge

A poem about marginalized young people. London is seen as a large machine they have learnt to play, but, for all their bravado and streetwise skill their hands are not on the 'controls' at Westminster.

How are the poem's vitality and edginess conveyed? What kind of imagery is used?

One Street Beyond

What is the effect of so many words ending in '-ing'? In what sense are the children *trackless* (2)? What is the poem's central message?

3 **skirmishing**   irregular, unpredictable fighting.

Rules for Beginners

A cautionary tale and a questioning of the messages we give one another. What standpoints do the different voices in the poem express? How should the mother's final comment be understood?

Two Women

The two are, in fact, one. The poem works by comparing the two types of work done by the same woman: *paid thinking/and clean hands* (1–2) and housework and caring for the family.

The image of *the simple, cool-skinned apples/of a father's loving objectivity* (12-13) is a crucial one. Why?

Ballad of the Morning After

Ballads are frequently thought-provoking; they present characters in predicaments which demand our imaginative involvement. The woman in this poem has taken her life into her own hands, unlike the woman in Gillian Clarke's *Overheard in County Sligo* whose approach has been more passive. The overwhelming impression we reach by the end of this ballad is that the woman has not 'got it right'. We can run an eye down the verses and guess where things 'went wrong'. There is no poet's 'persona' to give an answer, but the attitudes and observations the woman voices are familiar ones and encourage the reader to examine his or her own beliefs.

31 **Agape** Love feast held by early Chritians in connection with the Lord's Supper. The word comes from the Greek for brotherly love.

Eros sexual love.

32 **Utopian** ideally perfect.

36 **fraternity** brotherliness.

72 **PMT** pre-menstrual tension.

Gifts and Loans

This poem creates a record of a relationship which both people tacitly agree to limit, in spite of the happiness they find in each other's company. The voice in the poem knows everything about their relationship, even that they both realize that, were they to exchange their *adequate* (22) weekends for each other's company, they might still *end up with less* (24). The happiness expressed in this poem is worth comparing with the misery expressed in *Ballad of the*

Morning After. Commitment to values, loyalty, self-restraint, respect, consideration are seen to be worthwhile and important, giving the friends *simple space* (21), a quarrel-free relationship and much to savour.

A Marriage

This poem belongs with *Gifts and Loans* and shows how a writer can rework the same material. The two people are recognizably the same individuals, but this version offers more insight into the woman's mind, how she enters imaginatively into the family life of the man and how difficult she finds it to respond appropriately. Her strategy is to *become his child* (30), to deny the sexual attraction she may feel.

This poem raises some interesting questions and issues. Is the man telling 'the truth'? Is this picture of perfection to convince himself of his own good fortune? To strengthen their resolve to 'behave well'? His story certainly controls the woman's response, just as his own wife is enclosed within the home. But who is it who is conjuring her up embroidering, accepting *the perfect apple* (14) from her husband? Where does his 'story' end and the woman's imagination take over? Certainly the formality of the picture of the wife suggests the woman's imagination, particularly as the woman visualizes herself as the *dull cloth* (26) that allows the man to create his story.

The marriage, seen as a *small civilization* (6)—a microcosm, ties in well with the introduction of the Renaissance and the idea of decorum.

    7 **broadloom**   carpets woven at least 54 inches wide.
  16 **Renaissance**   In the Fourteenth to Sixteenth centuries there was a revival of arts and letters influenced by the Classical past. This revival is known as the Renaissance.

Unplayed Music

In this poem the piano, the tavern, and the landscape are all given human characteristics while people, apart from the man and woman, are simply *the crowd* (14). Why is this?

Days and Nights

A succession of pieces of information which prompt the reader to reflect. Which are the key phrases and how do they influence the reading of the poem?

    8 **the miracle of the loaves and fishes** Biblical tale of the feeding of the five thousand, when Jesus turned a few loaves and fishes into food enough for thousands.

Tides

   13 **malevolent** wishing evil on others.
   31 **valediction** a bidding farewell.

December Walk

   41 **Baroque** An artistic style of the Seventeenth and Eighteenth centuries involving plenty of decorative flourishes.

Carpet-weavers, Morocco

The children are seen as creating a world in the design of the carpet, creating a future and capturing the past. They are not merely children hard at work, but a part of the transmission of Islamic culture: *the garden of Islam grows* (5).

Selima Hill

Chicken Feathers

This long poem is made up of an apparently artless sequence of reminiscences about the poet's parents and moments in her childhood, culminating in a final section which reveals an acknowledgement that we only understand people, even parents, on our own terms, *My mother and I, in our way,/understand each other* (113–14). We read our own significance into moments, make meanings for ourselves to live with and by, but our perspective and understanding are not necessarily shared even by those closest to us. For example, the Mother, in Section XII, may not be waving after all, merely brushing away the feathers. How consoling is that?

The poem is far from artless: each section is clearly focused. Section I presents mother as a mythical figure, but in Section II she is disguised as a leopard about to fall under the spell of Harlequin. The meeting is 'mother's story', and it is clear in Section III that the relationship between mother and daughter, glimpsed at the school gates is awkward, distant. Section IV develops their separateness through physically distancing and contrasting both of them, mother in the garden watched by the child indoors and mother's cold hands contrasted with the child's warm ones.

By the time you reach the sections about father the theme of separateness is well established, separateness within families and the loss of contact death brings. The father's drawing and the poet's vision of the jetty are both attempts to imagine what death will be like, the former suggesting a solitary experience, a journey into a void; the latter hoping for a human welcome and sensory experience still.

Much of this poem's impact comes from the simplicity of the poet's voice, the confiding tone, the readiness to share imaginings that might invite ridicule or amusement, the moments of certainty and judgment that are later undercut by the realization that all may not be as it seems. The choice of detail – the tiny shoes, *like Cinderella's* (20), the moonlight as the chickens are put to bed, the orange peel, the *shining celandines* (109) – the mundane made significant, and the pictorial quality of each section, are other features that contribute to the success of this poem.

> 8 **Brunhilde** character in Wagner's *Ring Cycle* – a series of four operas. She was the favourite daughter of Wotan (King of the Gods), who earned her father's displeasure and was punished by being given to a mortal. A tragic and heroic figure.
> 59 **narcissi** scented, single white flower.
> 109 **celandines** bright yellow starlike woodland flower.

Dewpond and Black Drainpipes

The naïvety of the 'I' narrator, the choice of detail (the drying up cloth, the unromantic setting, the silence after the profession of love), help to make this a sadly comic poem. Mother has the last word.

> 18 **beatniks** defiantly unconventional young people whose manner of dress and 'modern' opinions shocked the older generations in the late 1950s.

Down by the Salley Gardens

The poem takes its title from an old song. The Irish poet, W. B. Yeats, was inspired to write it after hearing an old woman singing *Down by the Salley Gardens*. Compare Yeats' poem, below, with Selima Hill's.

Down by the Salley Gardens

Down by the Salley Gardens my love and I did meet;
She passed the Salley Gardens with little snow-white feet.
She bid me take love easy, as the leaves grow on the tree,
But I, being young and foolish, with her would not agree.

In a field by the river my love and I did stand,
And on my leaning shoulder she laid her snow-white hand.
She bid me take life easy, as the grass grows on the weirs;
But I was young and foolish, and now am full of tears.

Selima Hill's poem uses the song to reveal, by contrast, the 'you' in her poem. Once again the detail she uses is important: whether stamping the turf down or rubbing the back, muddy hands are a long way from snow-white feet and hands. The wedding photographs offer a further contrast. Is the children's action in leaving the photographs out deliberate? Is there any evidence that this woman's life may be *full of tears*?

The use of the present tense in *Darling, you are their bride* (13–14), as well as in verses 1 and 3, underlines the contrast being made.

What is the relationship between the two poems? Why should the voice in the poem be so protective of the 'you'?

159

The Goose

A poem about the meeting of cultures.

> 23 **Allah**   Muhammadans' name for God.

The Bicycle Ride

The ride, which begins with great enjoyment of the morning, does not lead to the *open country* (28) but becomes a reminiscence. The gathering after the funeral is made vivid by well chosen detail, the *sad unfamiliar aunts* (32), the *kind person* (37) who had made the tea, and the sandwiches shaped like the handerchiefs used by the father to dry his daughter's tears.

> 2 **First Communicant**   someone who has just made their First Communion, sharing in the symbolic reenactment of the Last Supper.

Diving at Midnight

This poem offers two perspectives on ways of attaining closeness to God. Once again, contrast is a significant feature of the poem: there is the girl for whom that closeness is exuberantly found in *the dive like a high note* (10–11), and the eskimo and his people who live *curled up, like the blue glass beads on the quiver* (49–51), enduring the polar landscape to achieve that closeness.

> 27 **Igjugarjuk**   An Inuit (Eskimo), who wrote an article about spiritual suffering.

Below Hekla

> 13–14 **Wilt Þú þissa, elskan,/þissa, þissa**   Do you want to have a pee?
>
> 33 **Barnaheimilið**   children's home

The Fowlers of the Marshes

Once again, the subject is the mother's strangeness and the complexity of the relationship between mother and daughter. What does the comparison with Ancient Egyptians permit the poet to say?

4 **faience**   decorated earthenware and porcelain.

6 **ibis**   stork-like bird found in lakes and swamps in warm climates. Worshipped by the Ancient Egyptians.

8 **Nut**   Earth Goddess, Ancient Egyptian Mistress of the Sky, Mother of the Sun. She swallowed the sun each night and gave birth to it again each morning. She was accompanied by vultures.

12 **Anubis**   Ancient Egyptian jackal god.

15 ***Thoth***   Ancient Egyptian God of Darkness, God of the Moon, Protector of the Dead. His symbols were the ibis and the baboon.

16 ***The Weighing of the Heart***   The Ancient Egyptians believed that after death the heart was weighed in scales against a feather, to judge its worth. (See *The Weighing of the Heart of the Scribe Ani* in the British Museum.)

Poems by Liz Lochhead

The Offering

The voice in the poem revisits her past. The 'would' of the first section becomes 'should' in the last: What might that imply? And why the title, *The Offering*? To what is the offering being made?

23–24 **Nicodemus**   an important Jewish teacher who came to consult Jesus under cover of night. (*St John* 8)

33 **Brethren**   religious community.

38 **Armageddon**   supreme conflict between nations (*Revelation* 16, 18).

45 **evangelist**   someone who preaches the gospel.

The Teachers

Like *The Offering*, this poem revisits the past by collecting together the attitudes, beliefs, and practices of the teachers, as noticed by a child. The overall impression is of a curious incoherence and mistaken certainties.

  13 **extolled**   praised enthusiastically.
  24 **tawse**   a slit thong for beating children.
  31 **helio**   mauve colour.

The Prize

An ironic reflection on prizes and being 'first'. The two perspectives, those of the child and an older person, are once again being used, as in *The Teachers* and *The Offering*.

Revelation

The contrast between inside the bull's shed and the benign farmyard is created economically and dramatically. Words like *reek* (9), *bulk* (11), *trampling* (12), *clanking* (12), *swivelled* (13), *tossed* (13) and *roared* (14) make the bull real and menacing – so that an interesting further development is possible in the second section, where he is turned into a representative of the forces of darkness, usually denied or kept at arm's length – a challenge to belief and civilization.

  21 **antidote**   medicine given to counteract poison.

Laundrette

A lively laundrette is transmuted into a poem of brief portraits, using vital and original vocabulary, rhyming, and word play. People *are* their laundry; their clothes in the machines behave like them.

  1 **nebulous**   cloudlike, hazy, vague.
  23 **fankle**   a Scottish dialect word, meaning 'tangle'.
  32 **flotsam**   wreckage found floating.

An Abortion

This poem has the unmistakable power of the eye-witness account, the unswerving eye, the recognition of suffering. The verbs used in the first section, *lolled* (6), *spiked* (7), *rolled* (7), *distended* (8) – words suggesting abnormality, are lifted onto a more anguished, symbolic plane by the reference to *Guernica* (see note on line 9). The men in blue – having distanced themselves from its suffering and tenderness, claim the beast *in the blue dusk* (57). The sounds of words, *hoick* (39), *long tongue… strong tongue* (47–48), *salt-lick* (50), *pumice* (50) help to make the event immediate and vivid.

  9 **Guernica**   Town in Northern Spain bombed by Fascists in the Spanish Civil War (1937). Picasso painted a large mural entitled *Guernica* in protest. It was the first major civilian blitz.

39 **hoick**   yank upwards.

50 **pumice**   light, spongy form of lava used for removing stains from hands.

Poppies

A poem that encourages the reader to reflect on people's sensitivities to the events marked by Remembrance Sunday. The last eight lines suggest a protest against the military's rituals that the more conventional members of society accept without question.

17 **forage cap**   cap worn by infantryman.

A Giveaway

  8 **felicity**   aptness.

The Other Woman

This poem, on first reading, uses the element of surprise, to subvert our expectations in the final section: *The other woman/lies/the other side of my very own mirror* (26–28). It is about the divided self, the ambivalence in relationships. What does the use of colloquial expressions contribute to the poem? It is quite a menacing poem – menacing towards the man, and unsettling in its admissions for the woman.

Storyteller

The poems on pages 132–35 come from a grouping called 'The Storyteller poems' which look at some of the elements of folk and fairy tales that virtually all children are told. They are stories with messages, both intended and unintended, which can influence people's views quite profoundly. The stories, *hung themselves upside down/in the sleeping heads of the children/till they flew again...* (27–29).

The first poem on page 132 presents the storyteller as a person with work to do, *It was like spinning* (16), but the stories are told at night and *fly again* at night like bats.

The Father and *The Mother* are composite portraits, showing what it is to be a father or mother in stories. How far do these notions of parenthood correspond with contemporary ideas of what one must be to be a good parent?

Spinster

4 **shards**   fragments of pottery.
8 **frugal**   careful, sparing.
　 circumspect   cautious, wary.

Everybody's Mother

This poem comes from a grouping called 'Hags and Maidens'. Is this a fair way of categorizing women? Does the picture of motherhood in this poem ring true for you? In which context might you come across the qualities presented in poem, e.g. adverts, magazines, films, soap operas?

50 **barrage balloon**   captive balloon which forms part of anti-aircraft defences during war.

Reviews

Gillian Clarke's poetry

In the reviews that follow, Gillian Clarke's achievement and standing as a contemporary poet is recognized in such phrases as: 'a poet with the craft and sensibility to claim herself an international reputation', 'accomplished', 'an important, vibrant voice', 'clarity of vision', and 'a seemingly natural gift for metaphor.' She is observed as being able to focus on small detail as well as being capable of taking on large themes and issues. She is seen as being 'earnest', 'honest', 'generous in [her] acceptance of the world' – an 'intuitive', 'instinctive' and 'accessible' writer.

Two reviewers seek to enhance her standing by suggesting points of similarity or indebtedness to Seamus Heaney and Ted Hughes, whose literary reputations have long been secure. Like Heaney, Clarke does mine family and cultural history; like Hughes, she does write about the natural world; but what is really interesting is the perspective from which and the way in which she writes about them. It is Anne Stevenson, in praising Clarke for her skill in presenting the 'private, personal, domestic' – 'a woman's view of what matters', who identifies and expresses a major preoccupation of Clarke's – that of recognizing the contribution women make to society and giving words 'to all human experience'. The poet as the 'voice of the tribe', as the giver of words to experiences we all share, as the recorder of 'true stories' – is the role Gillian Clarke takes on.

'The poem which lapses most completely into both nationalist and Romantic stereotypes is *Miracle on St David's Day*, when daffodils wave in mute admiration of an insane Welshman's recital of Wordsworth poem. I would rather stress the justly lauded title poem from *Letter from a Far Country* and the very fine lyrical pieces such as *Ram*, *Choughs*, and *The Water Diviner*. The influence of both Heaney and Hughes is clear, but it has been properly assimilated and informs some of her best work.

Poetry Review, Vol 73 No. 2, 1983

Of the new poems in this volume, Syphoning the Spring *and*
Overheard in County Sligo *are fine additions to her repertoire . . .*
The Selected Poems, *as a whole, display a poet with the craft and
the sensibility to claim herself an international reputation'.*

Poetry Review

'Selected Poems *is a rich, accomplished gathering, confirming
Gillian Clarke as an important, vibrant voice. She is not afraid of
approaching large themes; but life and death, love and loss, are
stations along a path she takes through the particular, the
familiar, the microcosm. Her language is a fine mesh of detail and
clarity.'*

Maura Dooley

'If Gillian Clarke has worked hard on these poems, signs of labour
are rarely evident. She has a seemingly natural gift for metaphor,
never allowing a poem to be overbalanced by an image and yet
getting the 'feel' exactly right... I don't think there exists a book
of poems today so abundant in its imagery or so generous in its
acceptance of the world as it is.

If there is fault to be found in these poems it is perhaps there is
too much abundance, too much acceptance. Like Peter
Redgrove, whom Gillian Clarke resembles in other ways, there is
little room to deal with evil in her vision of the world. Of sorrow,
however, she is unsparing. In one of her finest poems, *White Roses*
a boy is dying in a "green velvet sitting room" outside of which
"white roses bloom after rain." It is a scene painted by Bonnard,
bright, domestic in its details... The final stanza withdraws from
the scene with heartbreaking tact.

In poems like this about children, animals, life, death, Gillian
Clarke draws from the ancient springs of poetry without any
touch of sentimentality. How? How does she manage to treat
themes which so many other poets would ruin with overwriting
(or clever evasion) so directly and still move us? Perhaps it is
because she is perfectly honest and earnest about what she writes
as well as about the way she writes. Emphasis on technique and

originality among contemporary poets has occasioned a pervasive disregard of the obvious subjects. Or too often, a poet, fearful of generalizing, will confront us with details that are too private for communication. Gillian Clarke's poems are private, personal, domestic – and yet they generalize perpetually. Perhaps one definition of poetry would be "that form of language which best generalizes through the particular"... (of *Letter from a Far Country*) There is a frightening... expanse of time and space around this poem which will give the lie to any theory of women being able only to write small poems. And yet the poem is about small things – deliberately...

In a sense... by clinging to orthodoxies, by remaining a woman with a woman's view of what matters and what happens to people, [Gillian Clarke] has initiated a new form of 'feminism' which in no way attempts to compete with 'masculinism'... To my mind she has written a poem of the first political magnitude, as well as one of the great women's poems of any time.'
Anne Stevenson, The Powys Review, No. 17, 1985

'Because it has been done so well and so often by so many, a poetry based on natural description and response to the small everyday incidents of rural life invites failure in our time... To write firmly and steadily to a clarity of vision, with neither overreaching pretension nor inconsequential gabble, requires a poet of exceptional touch and tact, and Gillian Clarke is quite beautifully that poet...

She asserts from the outset that the presence of powerful natural forces is a confirmation of belief rather than a cause for doubt.'
Michael Hulse, Prospice 18, 1984

'She feels the power of fertility and the fragility of each individual life... The frequent conflict, of union and separateness characterizes her poems of personal relationship... The same duality defines her sense of the larger community.'
Jeremy Hooker, A Big Sea Running in a Shell: The poetry of
Gillian Clarke

'Where she lives, what she sees, hears, considers – the house, landscape and country she goes out from, and returns to – are Gillian Clarke's subjects... '

Pamela Stewart, *Planet*, October/November 1989

'Gillian Clarke writes of women *mixing rage with the family bread* (1. 364). The word *rage* is surprising because there is no rage in the poem... *Letter From a Far Country* is a love poem as well as a poem of anger and frustration... and the love prevents rage.'

Jeremy Hooker, *A Big Sea Running in A Shell: The Poetry of Gillian Clarke*

'Much is said by leaving the rest unsaid.'

Denis Donoghue, *London Review of Books*, 7 November 1985

Grace Nichols' poetry

Compared with some of the writers represented in this collection Grace Nichols has not received as much detailed critical attention from literary periodicals and the national-press. There are probably several reasons for this: her relatively recent appearance on the mainstream literary scene; her voicing of issues, concerns and experiences which, it may have been felt, would not be of immediate interest to a wide readership; and her use of Creole, which, on first reading, may present problems to those unfamiliar with its syntax and vocabulary.

Interestingly, the few reviews that go beyond introducing Grace Nichols and providing a lengthy quotation from one of her poems tend to focus on her language, rather than, as with the majority of other poets in this collection, their subject matter. What might have been mentioned was the importance of slavery and oppression in the poems, not just the oppression of black people by white – but also men's oppression of women. The strength and resourcefulness of the women who speak through the poems is one of the most remarkable and memorable aspects of Grace Nichols' work. They offer a sharp contrast with the warm, celebratory pictures of the Caribbean drawn from her memories of home and childhood.

In her introduction on pp. 31–33 Grace Nichols writes about wanting to 'fuse the two tongues', Creole and Standard English, because she comes from a background where 'the two worlds were constantly interacting'. This allows her to see the English language more objectively than many – and to weave into her poetry phrases for which Standard English has no equivalent. In essence, making language 'new' is what all good poets do – and Stewart Brown's fish simile is, in a nice way, saying just that. What neither of these reviewers address is the 'anguish and rage' referred to by James Berry, (in the introduction to his collection of West Indian Poetry, *News From Babylon*) which is a frequent feature of West-Indian-British poetry – and which Grace Nichols so concisely captures in the epilogue to *The Fat Black Woman's Poems*

I have crossed the ocean
I have lost my tongue
from the root of the old one
a new one has sprung.

'Grace Nichols' language is like those fish,' (in *Those Women*), lithe, shining, life-sustaining.'

'There is a distinctly sensual quality in much of the writing.'
Stewart Brown, *Poetry Review*

'By turns pungent and poignant, her poems enjoy calypso rhythms, Creole argot and streetwise London motifs...'
David Profumo

'Pleading the cause for free verse, although never openly, Grace Nichols uses everything which rightly belongs to this sort of verse... There are no villanelles, sonnets or other forms of English traditional poetry, and indeed, one feels closer to song or dance or the ballad in this alarming, freshly minted use of language and experience.'
Elizabeth Bartlett, *Poetry Review*, Vol. 79 No. 4, 1989

Fleur Adcock's poetry

As with the reviews on Gillian Clarke's writing, the reviewers of Fleur Adcock's poetry reveal uneasiness at individualism, autobiography and domesticity. Moreover, no debt to Heaney or Hughes can be claimed – she is described instead as 'the least fashion conscious of poets' who has 'shown a consistent disregard... for the prevailing literary models'. Stern comment, and one which might be understood as a lack of interest in the way others write. That is simply not so – she frequently writes reviews herself. Indeed the first reviewer, Dennis O'Driscoll, seems reluctant to praise at all. The choice of 'plain' to describe her style, rather than, perhaps 'direct', followed a little later by 'serviceable' and 'durable', suggests raincoats and lace-up shoes rather than language that captures experience and communicates insights. And it is the poems he feels fall short that are alluded to first, and his embarrassment at affection sincerely expressed. He concedes that Adcock writes 'ably' about children and adults, but once she turns her hand to global calamity or the death of a male friend he feels more reassured. Similarly, David Profumo, though more generous in his praise – 'a talented poet', 'excellent things on offer', 'psychology generally acute', 'unsettling wit' and 'dark shading' – sees the latter qualities giving way to 'a rag bag of offcuts'.

Just as Gillian Clarke's 'accessibility' might, one suspects, be held against her, the 'approachable' quality noted by Michael Hoffman in Fleur Adcock's writing, may be too. His choice of the words 'neat' and 'lively', followed by 'clean-minded' trivializes the seriousness and perceptiveness of Adcock's work. 'Bland' and 'underpowered' are further blows, mitigated only by his observation that she has 'a gift for direct statement and discomfiting truth'.

There is a clear, distinctive voice in Fleur Adcock's poetry, excellent use of dialogue and the dramatic moment, acute observation of people and situations and a political awareness for which these reviewers offer her no credit. That her subject matter is often close to home is immaterial. She, like Gillian Clarke, wants to communicate rather than to impress, astound, intrigue or fascinate.

'Fleur Adcock is the least fashion-conscious of poets. She has shown a consistent disregard, over the years, for the prevailing literary models, and her plain, ironic, humane style, which has proved so serviceable and durable, owes no obvious debt to anyone... Her 'one prescription' for a poem is very simple: 'it's got to be good.''

'Not all her poems are good, of course. She can sound too knowing sometimes and there are occasions when her plainness slides into flatness. In *The Incident Book...* the poems in the *Schools* section are among those which fail to rise above a forgettable flatness. Elsewhere, however... Adcock's ability to convey a child's-eye view of the world has been a distinctive and charming feature of her output...'

'Adcock writes ably about adults as well as children and she addresses an affectionate and affecting poem, *The Chiffonier* to her mother. Though marred by the bathos of certain lines... a vivid portrait emerges. *The Keepsake* is a more skilful poem which undergoes a deft and shocking transformation from joy in a friend's presence to shock at his absence.'

'Her calm, almost leisurely tone chillingly intensifies the horror of sudden disasters and global calamity, (*Last Song*) where a more strident voice would have failed.'

Dennis O'Driscoll, *Poetry Review*, Vol. 77 No. 1, 1987

'Adcock is a talented poet, but there are too many places where her qualities of unsettling wit and dark shading have given way to a ragbag of offcuts... There are some excellent things on offer and the psychology is generally acute.'

David Profumo, *Sunday Times*, 22 February 1987

'The poems are neat, lively, approachable, clean-minded . . . Adcock's tone, bland and reasonable and underpowered is quite attractive on its own – but the poems seem to be falling over themselves... Adcock's gift is for direct statement and surprising or discomfiting truth.'

Michael Hoffman, *Times Literary Supplement*, 13 February 1987

Carol Rumens' poetry

Of the critics quoted below, David Profumo's observation that
Carole Rumens gives voice to the 'multiple tensions' of modern
living is one of the most helpful. More than Selima Hill, Fleur
Adcock or Gillian Clarke, she focuses on public and private
morality, her eye perceives and then her conscience closes in.
Sometimes she reveals a dilemma and its resolution, sometimes she
assembles her observations and lets the reader draw the conclusions.

Her humane, compassionate standpoint is rather unfairly des-
cribed by George Szirtes as 'a kind of moral adolescence'. He is
charitable enough to list what he feels to be many sterling qualities
but baulks at the 'subject matter and the emotion applied to it'.
More to the point, though, is the uncertainty of purpose and focus
in the poem to which he refers. At her best, Rumens does not leave
us with uncertainty.

In her introduction on pp. 73–75, Rumens comments on the
pitfalls of writing political poetry. Yet her political poems, flawed
though some may be, give a sense of late Twentieth century living in
a way that those of no other poet in this collection do. Similarly her
use of traditional structures with contemporary diction, though
awkward at times, make for arresting and thought-provoking poems.

'She confronts painful experience with balance and control.

… her readiness to enter other lives… One of the finest younger
poets writing in England today.'
Elaine Feinstein, *Times Literary Supplement*, 20th November 1987

'… a kind of moral adolescence lights up the oeuvre… a
temperament seeking for a "just cause" which would enable it
properly to express itself.'

'… a writer split between two worlds: her language is intelligent,
observant, sometimes witty, even humorous, formally controlled,
compassionate and… essentially romantic. What gives us pause
is her subject matter and the emotion applied to it. The moral eye
presented by the poems is not always convincing. Take *Ballad of*

the Morning After, ostensibly about personal love. Of its twenty verses, seven deal with social comment and ideology, fine in their way, but diffusing the effect of the other thirteen...
Nevertheless, Carol Rumens is a very good poet.'

George Szirtes, *Poetry Review*, Vol. 77 No. 3, 1977

' ...a writer giving voice to the multiple tensions with which... we have to live.'

David Profumo, *Sunday Times*, 9th March 1987

Selima Hill's poetry

It is a good reviewer who can illuminate as well as pass judgment or recommend, and Selima Hill has, on the whole, fared well at the hands of her reviewers. Why this should be is, at first glance, something of a mystery. Much of her writing is domestic in focus, autobiographical, full of strange mythological allusions and apparently naïve in tone – a potential target for a close, critical shot. However her quiet, confiding voice 'takes you into her life', makes a companion of you, and convinces you that her writing is finely calculated, as well as being bizarre and persistently haunting. Rosemary Hill makes the observation that Selima Hill is one of the few poets genuinely interested in the different experiences of men and women, and there are indeed many times in the poems when a moment in a relationship between a man and a woman is brought fleetingly, yet sharply, into focus. Her detachment is the key to her understanding, and gives the impression of 'cool, elegant poise.' It also permits satire.

At the same time there is an awareness that detachment does not necessarily lead to full enlightenment. Can we trust our perceptions? How accurate is our understanding of the world we inhabit? The tentativeness and lack of insistence noted by Neil Corcoran, may be a distancing device from 'panic, misgiving and disgust'. It may simply arise from a recognition that life is far more mysterious than we normally care to acknowledge. 'I do not want to judge,' Hill writes in her introduction on pp. 99–100, 'but to be still and understand'.

'Selima Hill is a companionable poet... she takes you into her life.'
'She is 'one of the few writers interested in the different experiences of men and women'.

Rosemary Hill, *Poetry Review*, Vol. 78 No. 3, 1988

Hill's is a voice, 'tentative and uninsistent' with a 'cool elegant poise. The point about the cool elegant poise... of all this however, is that it is always shadowed by something which is not poise at all, but panic, misgiving and disgust. The art with which these are kept in check gives the poems their characteristic, edgy pathos.'

'Hill exhibits a 'self-deprecating, wary sadness.'

'She has a way of 'making the contemporary, not the historical seem remote.'

'Weirdly detached humour... There is something of Stevie Smith in this, but Selima Hill is more calculating in her use of whimsy and more controlled in her rhythms.'

'Her solipsism is just as desolate and convincing as Smith's, but also more casual and resigned.'

The Ram is a 'sharp, satiric comedy.'

Neil Corcoran, *Times Literary Supplement*, 7 September 1984

'Selima Hill's poetry is receding further and further into a world of dreamlike mystery. Events, characters and settings are often baffling... but, as in dreams, the details are solid and of the real world, and the tone is matter-of-fact and unsurprised... It is the apparent normality of bizarre events which makes these poems work: they have an extraordinary innocence of tone... to call it 'naivety', which is tempting, would be to ignore the undoubted sophistication of the writing... lyrical precision and an acute, filmic eye for self-contained episodes... make the best of the poems... so irresistible'.

Fleur Adcock, *The Times Literary Supplement*

Liz Lochhead's poetry

Once again the adjective *domestic* is one of the first chosen to describe the work of a female poet by a male reviewer. But there are many ways of being domestic, and the way home issues and activities are handled by Gillian Clarke is very different from their treatment at the hands of Liz Lochhead. It is the archetype that is the central feature of several poems as Liz Lochhead herself observes in her introduction on pp. 117–119. As for the phrase, *with a-vengeance*, perhaps it should be countered with the question, 'in what sense?' Perhaps it does still need asserting that things domestic are just as worthy of the pen as anything else. It is also interesting to note that her writing is deemed to have 'gained authority' once she has moved on from 'the nature of feminity and the complexity of relationships'.

An important characteristic of Liz Lochhead's work is its dramatic quality. Voices speak clearly through the poems, characters emerge, judgements are made, predicaments explored. Many of them make superb performance pieces, or work well simply read out loud. They challenge and speak for others – and it is often the *status quo* in relationships, or what often goes unquestioned, that is challenged.

'A domestic poet with a-vengeance... ' in her earlier works 'the main themes are the nature of femininity and the complexity of *relationships* – but the writing has gained authority and the voice of the poet is more distinctive.'

'Almost all the poems have romance in the background.'

'The weaving in of... folklore adds extra depth and often enables the poet to be involved and detached.'

James Campbell, *Times Literary Supplement*, 15 May 1981

Further Reading

Gillian Clarke

Sundial, J. D. Lewis, 1978.
Letter from a Far Country, Carcanet, 1982.
Selected Poems, Carcanet, 1985.
Letting in the Rumour, Carcanet, 1989.
Harvest at Mynachlog, Gwasg Gregynog, 1990.
The King of Britain's Daughter, Carcanet, 1993.

Grace Nichols

Trust you, Wriggly!, Hodder, 1981.
Leslyn in London, Hodder, 1984.
Fat Black Woman's Poems, Virago, 1984.
Dangerous Knowing, Sheba Feminist Publishers, 1984.
Whole of a Morning Sky, Virago, 1986.
Lazy Thoughts of a Lazy Woman, Virago, 1989.
Poetry Jump Up (ed.), illustrated by Michael Levy, Puffin, 1990.

Fleur Adcock

Selected Poems, OUP (NZ), 1985.
The Incident Book, Oxford Publishers, OUP, 1986.
Hotspur, G. Albrecht Paperback Bloodaxe Books, 1986.
Meeting the Comet, Paperback Bloodaxe Books, 1988.
Manchester Poetry, (ed.), Paperback Manchester Poets, 1989.
Time-zones, Oxford Poets' Society, OUP (NZ), 1991.

Carol Rumens

Selected Poems, Chatto, 1987.
Making for the Open, Chatto, 1987.
Greening of the Snow Beach, Paperback Bloodaxe Books, 1988.
From Berlin to Heaven, Chatto, 1989.
New Women Poets, (ed.), Paperback Bloodaxe Books, 1990.
Thinking of Skins, Bloodaxe Books, 1993.

Selima Hill

Saying Hello at the Station, Chatto, 1984.
My Darling Camel, Chatto, 1988.
The Accumulation of Small Acts of Kindness, Chatto, 1989.
A Little Book of Meat, Bloodaxe Books, 1993.

Liz Lochhead

Dreaming Frankenstein and Collected Poems, Polygon Books, 1984.
True Confessions and New Clichés, Polygon Books, 1984.
Tartuffe, Polygon, 1986.
Mary Queen of Scots Got Her Head Chopped Off and Dracula, Penguin, 1989.
Bagpipe Muzack, Penguin, 1991.

Anthologies featuring these poets

Allnutt, D'Aguiar, and Mottram Edwards, eds.: *The New British Poetry*, Paladin, 1988.
J. Berry: *News From Babylon*, Chatto & Windus, 1984
P. Burnett, ed.: *The Penguin Book of Caribbean Verse in English*, Penguin, 1986.
S. and A. Brownjohn, eds.: *Meet and Write*, Hodder & Stoughton, 1987.
J. Couzyn, ed.: *The Bloodaxe Book of Contemporary Women Poets*, Bloodaxe Books, 1985.
L. France, ed.: *Sixty Women Poets*, Bloodaxe Books, 1993.

Critical works

Poetry Review, Vol. 73, No. 2, 1983: M. O'Neill on Gillian Clarke; James Berry on West-Indian/British poetry; Vol. 74, No. 2, 1984 Terry Eagleton on Grace Nichols; Vol. 74, No. 3, Marion Shaw on Grace Nichols; Vol. 78 No. 3, 1988 Rosemary Hill on Selima Hill.

Tasks

1 Consider the way in which any two poets from this collection write about family relationships. What ground do they share as far as subject matter and use of language are concerned? How does their work differ?

2 After looking closely at the work of two poets, design two covers for collections of their poetry closely based on the poets' themes, ideas, images and language. Write explaining the process by which you arrived at your designs. How well, in your opinion do the covers illuminate the poems? What aspects of the poets' work did you find hardest to capture – and why?

3 Discuss the ways in which religious belief appears and is explored in this collection.

4 Consider the ways in which domestic detail is used by these writers – and to what effect?

5 Make a selection of poems from this collection which lend themselves particularly well to performance. Which qualities are the ones you identified in order to make your selection? Create a script for a programme which introduces the poems and provides a commentary where appropriate. Stage the reading/performance, evaluate, and report on it. What more did you learn about the poems from this staging? How does the experience of listening to poems differ from the experience of reading to oneself?

6 The poet, Fred D'Aguiar, has written that in selecting poems for a collection he edited he was 'looking for a true tone and a sense that the poet had wrapped his or her mind around the subject, holding it in a vice-steady grip long enough to reveal something not seen before.' Which poems in this collection have impressed you in this way – and why? What contribution does the writers' technique make to this freshness of vision?

7 Discuss the images of motherhood in this collection and the way in which these images have been created.

8 How do the poets in this collection depict romantic love? What common ground do they share and how does their work differ?

9 Which of these poets have you found most rewarding to study – and why?

10 Titles can be important. Discuss any three poems which have in your opinion either particularly significant or particularly unhelpful titles. Be sure to justify your opinions by referring to the texts.

11 From this collection of poetry, which images of the late Twentieth century emerge most clearly? How are these images created – and are they the images you would have chosen yourself:

12 Several of the poems in this collection are concerned with justice. Discuss the poets' treatment of the theme drawing attention to the poems' similarities and differences. What is being said about our society and how persuasive do you find the poems?

13 Challenging the *status quo* and challenging assumptions runs throughout this collection. Are poems the appropriate form for this? Argue your case by using references from the poems.

14 If you were to be allowed only three poems from this collection to keep with you during a long, enforced period of isolation, which poems would they be and why?

15 A sense of history runs through this collection. How do these poets see the past? What significance does it hold for them – and how do they weave it into their poems?

16 How do the women poets in this collection depict men? Support your observations with close textual reference.

17 Philip Larkin in *Required Writing* has asserted that the pleasure principle should be applied to poetry; that poetry reading should compete with other forms of recreation. Select 3 poems which, for you, might successfully outweigh a night out at the cinema or a good meal in terms of pure enjoyment and time well spent. Explain your choices, being sure to refer closely to the poems themselves.

18 In your opinion, are the poems in this collection weighted too heavily on the serious side? Comment on the balance of the comic and serious with close reference to specific poems.

19 Stories of many kinds fill the pages of this collection. Retell any

two in prose and compare them with the original poems. Comment on the gains and losses of the genre switch and comment on what you have learnt about the poets' use of language in the process.

20 Discuss the images of school and the child's experience of school in the collection. What are the similarities and differences that come into focus? Look closely at the language the poets use.

Index of Titles and First Lines